THE BAYFRONT

BOOK

COASTAL HISTORIES BY
STEVE M. WYATT

EDITED BY
CATHERINE A. NOAH

OREGON COAST
HISTORY CENTER

OLDTOWN PRINTERS

The Bayfront Book is one of more than thirty books and videos published by the Lincoln County Historical Society since it was founded in 1948. Research and images for this book came from the Society's vast archives, which include thousands of historic photographs, news clippings, maps, and other documents. These materials are available to the public for research purposes. The Society's research library and two museums, the Burrows House and Log Cabin, are located at the Oregon Coast History Center, 545 S.W. Ninth St., Newport, Oregon, 97365.

TABLE OF CONTENTS

FORWARD

Few regions enjoy as much interest in local history as the central Oregon Coast. Spurring this interest is the monthly publication of *The Bayfront* magazine. *The Bayfront*'s lively and well-researched articles, combined with a generous complement of historic photographs, have made it a favorite among locals and visitors alike. Devoted readers continually seek out the latest edition to find out what's new in history.

Since its 1991 debut, readership of *The Bayfront* magazine has increased tremendously. Each year, well over 50,000 copies are distributed throughout the central Oregon Coast by its publisher, Oldtown Printers. It is probably the most widely read magazine in the region. Countless back issues continue to recirculate as they are passed along and mailed to history buffs all over the world. Some editions of *The Bayfront* have been known to be sold at garage sales.

This collection contains twenty-two selected stories from *The Bayfront* magazine written from 1993 to 1998 by Steve M. Wyatt, curator of the Oregon Coast History Center. For this special edition, Wyatt reedited and in many cases expanded upon the original articles, thanks to additional information submitted by *Bayfront* readers. Space limitations did not permit the inclusion of every magazine story and photograph in this edition.

Information and images for these stories came from the research library of the Oregon Coast History Center, administered by the Lincoln County Historical Society, in Newport, Oregon. This facility is the largest repository of information and photographs pertaining to the central Oregon Coast. Each year, hundreds of people take advantage of its ever-expanding archives. The History Center's collection consists of thousands of photographs, newspapers on microfilm, books, maps, family histories, business records, and other materials pertaining to the history of the region.

This book is dedicated to the countless people who have graciously shared their family heirlooms, photographs, and stories with the Oregon Coast History Center. The center's museum exhibits, publications, videos, library, and programs would not be possible without the willingness of people to share their treasures with others.

LORETTA HARRISON,
EXECUTIVE DIRECTOR,
OREGON COAST HISTORY CENTER

THE BAYFRONT BOOK

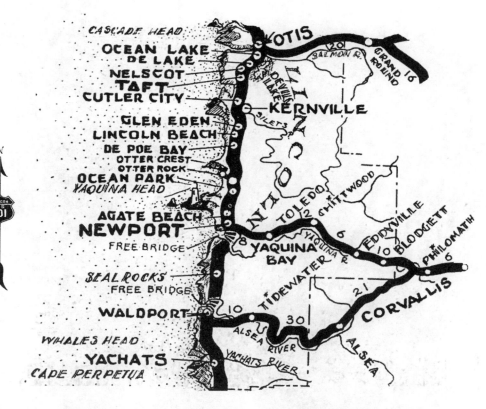

*Lincoln County, detail from a map in "Travel Oregon Coast Highway"
brochure by the Oregon Coast Highway Association, 1936.*

Yaquina Bay commercial oysterman.

Opposite: Digging for rock oysters, 1910s. (A.L. Thomas)

HISTORY ON THE HALF SHELL

EARLY DAY YAQUINA BAY

Lewis, Winant, Ludlow, and Wachsmuth are not names most people would associate with the fast-food industry. But in the 1800s, these names — all connected with Yaquina Bay — were tied closely with one of America's most popular fast foods: oysters. Nationwide restaurant chains offering hamburgers and tacos on demand were decades away; 19th-century restaurants were locally owned and operated, and if a hungry customer was in a hurry, oysters were in order.

The nation's insatiable demand for oysters spurred the settlement of this region in the early 1860s when rich oyster beds were discovered in Yaquina Bay. The quest for Yaquina Bay oysters, a unique, succulent variety called *Ostrea lurida*, changed this region forever.

Claims to when the Yaquina Bay oyster beds were discovered and by whom are nearly as numerous as the oysters were in the 1860s. Few could argue the first ones to "discover" oysters in the bay were the Native Americans,

who had inhabited the area for thousands of years prior to the arrival of Euro-Americans. Without a doubt, the resident Yacona Indians knew about the oysters, but archaeological evidence indicates they favored a diet of fish (primarily salmon), clams, and mussels.[1]

THE LEWIS FAMILY: EARLY OYSTER EATERS

Perhaps the first residents to include Yaquina Bay oysters as a regular part of their diet were Joseph B. Lewis and family. Lewis came to Yaquina Bay in 1855 with his wife, Lucy Metcalf, a Tututni Indian from the lower Rogue River.[2] Lewis probably came as an employee of the Siletz Indian Reservation, which was established that year. One day in 1856, family members were using a dugout canoe for fishing and clamming when they came across the oysters.[3] Lewis spent the rest of his life in the oyster business. In 1871, he officially homesteaded the land where Oysterville

Below: Oysterville, ca. 1890.

Opposite: Capt. J.J. Winant, prior to 1894. (Bradley & Rulofson)

eventually would be located. When he died, his oyster beds were passed on to his son, George (1871-1956), who was born in Oysterville and also spent his life in the oyster business. In 1932, the Lewis family had control of twenty-three acres of oyster beds.[4] George recalled in 1948, "I was only seven when I helped prepare the now-famous little Yaquina Bay oysters to be sent to San Francisco. This was the first cash business our bay ever had, and for many years the business flourished. Yaquina Bay oysters were a famed dish at the Waldorf-Astoria in New York and at the finest hotels in San Francisco."[5]

WINANT AND LUDLOW: OYSTER PURVEYORS

When word of the rich oyster beds on Yaquina Bay (still part of the Siletz Indian Reservation) reached California in the early 1860s, two San Francisco businesses, Winant and Co. and Ludlow and Co., took an interest.

Capt. J.J. Winant (1838-1894) was the pilot of the first steam-powered vessel to enter Yaquina Bay.[6] He entered into a business relationship with Joseph Lewis[7] and stationed his representative, Capt. Solomon Dodge, to establish a presence on what became the site of Oysterville, Yaquina Bay's first town. When Royal A. Bensell, who would become a founding father of Newport, visited Oysterville, he described it as situated on a steep bluff overlooking Yaquina Bay. Below were floats and boats crowded with Siletz Indian women engaged in culling or sorting work for which they were paid twelve-and-a-half cents a bushel.[8] In addition to paying the workers, Winant and Co. compensated the Siletz Indian Reservation fifteen cents per bushel in exchange for use of the oyster beds.[9]

The other San Francisco operation, Ludlow and Co., took a more brazen approach: it claimed it was the right of all Americans to fish American waters. Ludlow

Winant and Co.'s Mischief *on the Bayfront, July 23, 1889. Captain Winant is standing center with his hand on the sail. (Morrison)*

employees were arrested and removed from the bay. The courts ultimately ruled against the company and upheld the Winant lease. While its case was pending, Ludlow still managed to ship several cargoes of oysters to San Francisco.[10]

Capt. J.J. Winant's Mischief, ca. 1890. (Winter & Brown)

While the Ludlow venture was short-lived, the Winant operation remained active for two decades. It harvested Yaquina Bay oysters by the boatload and sold them in San Francisco until the mid-1880s. By 1885, the town of Oysterville had begun to decline.[11] With the exception of one building, Oysterville was destroyed by fire in August 1889.[12]

After Capt. Winant left the oyster trade, he remained active in the area's shipping business. In 1886, he had the freighter *Mischief* built at Yaquina.[13] The arrival of the *Mischief* was a frequent sight in just about every Oregon and Washington port of the day. Later Winant took control of the steamer *Bonderville*. In 1894, Winant was swept off *Bonderville*'s deck and drowned in waters near Gardiner, Oregon.[14]

WACHSMUTH: WINANT'S LEGACY

While Winant left the oyster trade never to return, one of his ex-employees came back to the business in a big way. Meinert Wachsmuth had visited Yaquina Bay in 1865 as a crew member aboard the *Annie Doyle*, a steamer in the Winant fleet. The boat wrecked on Yaquina Bay. Wachsmuth survived; he lost his taste for the seafaring life but not his appetite for seafood. Wachsmuth left Winant and Co. to work oyster beds in Willapa Harbor, Washington. Wachsmuth must have told his son, Louis (1877-1957), of the rich Yaquina oyster beds, because Louis went on to form the Oregon Oyster Co. in 1927 and acquire the beds not far from the Oysterville of old. Louis grew an imported oyster rather than the Yaquina Bay variety, which

Louis Wachsmuth, center, packing oysters sometime in the 1930s.

had become nearly extinct. Louis regarded his oysters as the best in the world and used them in his famous stews and cocktails at his landmark Portland restaurant, Dan & Louis' Oyster Bar.[15] The Wachsmuth family retained ownership of the Yaquina Bay oyster beds until 1993, when the beds were sold to the Newport-based Oregon Pacific Corporation,[16] which later became known as the Yaquina Bay Oyster Company.

As early as 1869, concerns were raised over the depletion of the Yaquina Bay oyster beds. The oystermen banded together to form the Yaquina Bay Oyster Protective Association.[17] More recently, biologists at Newport's Hatfield Marine Science Center and the Oregon Department of Fish and Wildlife have worked to save the *Ostrea lurida* (the last native oysters left on the Oregon

Coast) from extinction.[18]

Before the discovery of the oyster beds, the outside world knew almost nothing of the region. Those who knew of the central Oregon Coast held it in low regard, primarily because of its isolation. But when the oyster business boomed in the 1860s, a wagon road was built to Yaquina Bay from Corvallis. With the area no longer isolated, entrepreneurs pressured the U.S. government to open it up to Euro-American settlement. In January 1866, the Yaquina Bay, which included lands north to Cape Foulweather and south to Alsea Bay, was opened for settlement. Most of the settlers were ex-employees from the Siletz Reservation. With settlement came depletion of the native oyster beds and development of other industries heavily dependent on

Oystermen on Yaquina Bay, ca. 1890. Across the river is West Yaquina.

Oregon Oyster Company, 1970s. (News-Times)

Opposite: Tonging for oysters on Yaquina Bay, 1973.

the coast's natural resources: wood products, fishing, and tourism. These changes may have occurred without the discovery of Yaquina Bay oysters, but America's desire for a quick bite to eat probably accelerated the development of Yaquina Bay considerably.

END NOTES
1. E. Wayne Courtney, *The Indians of Yaquina Bay* (Corvallis: Sanderling Press, 1989), 8.
2. "Old Timer Has Birthday," *Yaquina Bay News*, 30 March 1927.
3. Joe Lewis, typed summary of an interview by Rosa Claridge, undated, from Oregon Coast History Center collection.
4. Untitled, *Portland Journal*, 19 April 1932, typed version by

Evelyn Parry.

5. "Chamber Hears About Bay Oysters," *Newport News*, 19 Aug. 1948.

6. "Swept from the Deck," news clipping, unidentified paper dated 1894, from Oregon Coast History Center collection.

7. George Lewis obituary, *Yaquina Bay News*, 01 May 1947.

8. Royal A Bensell, *All's Quiet on the Yamhill: The Civil War in Oregon* (Eugene: University of Oregon Books, 1959), 125.

9. David F. Fagan, *History of Benton County, Oregon* (Portland: A.G. Walling, Printer, 1885), 480.

10. Ibid., 480-484.

11. Ibid., 490.

12. "Oysterville Burned," *Corvallis Gazette*, 09 Aug. 1889.

13. "The New Coasting Steamer *Mischief*," *Corvallis Gazette*, 06 Aug. 1886.

14. "Swept from the Deck."

15. Dan & Louis' Oyster Bar menu, 1986, Oregon Coast History Center collection.

16. "Oregon Oyster Rich in History," *News-Times*, Feb. 1995.

17. Fagan, 485.

18. "Native Oysters Make Comeback Along Oregon Coast," *Oregonian*, 18 Feb. 1997.

NEWPORT: BORN ON THE FOURTH OF JULY

July 4, 1866: the 90th anniversary of declared American independence, a perfectly legitimate reason to throw a party on the Yaquina Bay. The only known account of this historical gathering appears in *The History of Benton County, Oregon*, written by David F. Fagan in 1885. The celebration started with the rising of the sun in Pioneer City,[1] where seventy-five passengers boarded the steamer *Pioneer* and headed down the Yaquina River, stopping at Elk City, Toledo, Oysterville, Oneatta, and other towns to pick up more partyers. Their destination was a place called North Beach, just below where the Yaquina Bay Coast Guard Station is today. By the time the *Pioneer* arrived, the gathering was seven hundred strong. This included 300 residents from the Siletz Indian Reservation.[2]

Such an event would have been impossible a few months earlier. From 1855 to 1866, the bay officially was closed to non-Indian settlement as it was part of the 1.3 million-acre Siletz Indian

Reservation.[3] At the time of this gathering, the Yaquina Bay area had been open for settlement a mere six months. Sam Case (1831-1897), an ex-employee of the reservation, took out a land claim that included North Beach and much of the land that is now Newport. Case and his partner, Dr. James R. Bayley (1820-1901), constructed the Ocean House Hotel where the Coast Guard Station stands today. The Ocean House was completed in April 1866. Besides commemorating the fourth of July, this may have been a grand opening celebration for the Ocean House and a kickoff for Newport's first-ever tourist season.

For this gathering, a tall flag pole was installed at a spruce grove on the Ocean House grounds especially for an American flag presented by the delegation representing the ladies of Corvallis. The "informal proceedings" continued with singing and speeches that "teemed with loyalty, patriotism, and eloquence." The flag was then hoisted up the

Ocean House, 1860s. Sam Case is leaning against the post at center.

pole and the Declaration of Independence read aloud.

Perhaps inspired by the reading of this democratic document, the settlers of Yaquina Bay voted to avail themselves to all laws of the United States as of July 1, 1864. Then the name "Newport" was chosen for the town site where the revelers stood. No one knows for a fact who named the town, but it is commonly believed it was Sam Case. Not only is he regarded as the town's founder, he was raised near a resort town in Rhode Island called Newport where there was a famous hotel called the Ocean House. A slogan also was chosen. It was not "The Friendliest," but a slightly less-catchy designation, "the 'germ' of the San Francisco of Oregon." The celebration then broke up at the respectable hour of four in the afternoon.[4]

Although Newport had a name in 1866, it was not really a town. Without jetties, entering the bay was difficult at best. Major shipping and fishing industries were decades

Two early images of Newport: The beach and Ocean House (left), and the Bayfront looking east, both ca. 1880. (J.G. Crawford)

Newport may or may not have been named when this photo was taken, sometime in 1865-66. The buildings are Livingston's Cake and Beer Shop and Butch Hammer's Card & Whiskey Saloon.

away. Few tourists were willing to endure the trek to Newport, which required an all-day wagon ride from Corvallis, a night in Elk City, and a twenty-five-mile mail boat ride the next day.[5] Oysterville, located upriver from Newport in close proximity to rich oyster beds, was the hub of what little business activity the bay supported.

The dream of prosperity on the bay was still alive, however. In 1868, the government completed a survey of the harbor and found it was deeper than expected.[6] Talk of Newport becoming a major seaport began to circulate. In 1881, the federal government began construction on the south jetty.[7] The prospect of large ocean-going ships carrying goods in and out of Yaquina Bay put Newport on the map. Colonel T. Egenton Hogg and his investors decided to build a railroad line to Yaquina Bay that would carry both tourists and freight for the ships docking there. Growth and speculation on the bay grew at a feverish pace. It was thought that Yaquina Bay would be a shopping destination for residents of the Willamette Valley who did not want to travel all the way to Portland for supplies.

By the latter part of 1882, Newport had incorporated. The town needed an infrastructure and improvements to deal with the anticipated growth. Alonzo Case (1844-1920), nephew of Sam Case, was elected council president (mayor). At the City Council's first meeting in November 1882, Ordinance Number One was passed. The ordinance declared that no one could sell liquor or spirits in quantities of less than one quart without getting a license from the City Council. Immediately after its passage, the City executed what may have been its first transaction: a liquor license sold to B.E. Gardner for one hundred dollars.

Evidently crime was also a concern that day: the council voted to accept bids for a jail. By the next meeting it had received two bids, both of which were thrown out because they were too high ($190 and $200). Marshall Callamore was sent to a sawmill at Oneatta (where River Bend Moorage is today) to purchase $33.31 worth of lumber and $17.75 of nails and other materials. Callamore may have built the jail; he was given an extra $8.50 for his service.[8]

Crime was not the only problem. The infant town of Newport also had to deal with traffic, even though it had no streets (except one, if you counted the beach). In 1882, the City Council set out to alleviate this problem. It advised

All the necessities: Newport's C.H. Williams store (dry goods, groceries, and post office) and Eugene Williams' Cem Saloon, on First (Front) Street. (J. G. Crawford)

all property owners to remove their buildings facing the bay. A wooden bulkhead was then constructed along the bay in front of the town for three blocks. With completion of the bulkhead in April 1883, Front Street became a three-block-long thoroughfare. The rest of Front Street remained the beach.[9]

As the town developed, so did new businesses. In 1882, a brewery was built near Newport. The Ocean House and the Bay View Hotel (later known as the Abbey) made substantial additions to accommodate the influx of tourist traffic. Shops, livery stables, and houses appeared on the Bayfront.[10] By 1890, the population of Newport had boomed to 121 inhabitants.[11] A rival town, Yaquina City, sprang up at the end of the railroad line six miles east. Within a short time, Yaquina's population tripled Newport's.

During the 1880s, local residents believed that with the completion of the railroad and jetty, Yaquina Bay would become a major shipping port overnight. This was not to be. In 1887, the railroad's steamer, *Yaquina City*, which carried freight and offered passenger connections to San Francisco, went aground near the South Jetty and broke up. It was replaced with the steamer *Yaquina Bay*, which wrecked entering the bay. The two shipwrecks, combined with financial difficulties, led to the sale of the railroad. The dream of Yaquina Bay becoming a major shipping port

A wooden bulkhead built in 1883 provided Newport with its first street (that wasn't a beach). (Crawford & Paxton)

190 NEWPORT FROM BULKHEAD.

with Yaquina City as its hub was abandoned.

Despite these setbacks, the railroad remained in operation under a series of owners. Instead of freight, the railroad carried primarily passengers drawn to the coast by sandy beaches and fresh salt air. With the railroad running, Newport was an easy five-hour trip for Willamette Valley tourists. Yaquina City faded away as there was no reason for travelers to linger there except to catch a ferry ride into Newport. Although his town did not become San Francisco, Sam Case's July Fourth dream of a thriving West Coast resort town called Newport was realized.

Above: Members of the Siletz tribe dance on the Bayfront during what was probably Fourth of July, ca. 1912.

Opposite: Fourth of July parade down the Bayfront, 1911.

END NOTES

1. Dr. George Kellogg established this town earlier that same year two miles upriver from Elk City; by the 1880s, this place was all but a ghost town. In the 1890s, it became the center for rock quarry activity and in 1894 was renamed Morrison when a post office was established there.

2. David F. Fagan, *History of Benton County, Oregon* (Portland: A.G. Walling, Printer, 1885), 487-488.

3. William Eugene Kent, *The Siletz Indian Reservation 1855-1900* (Newport: Lincoln County Historical Society, 1977), 1-2.

4. Fagan, 488.

5. C.E. Carr, "Early Days on Yaquina Bay," *Oregon Journal*, 28 Jan. 1913.

6. Richard L. Price, *Newport, Oregon 1866-1936, Portrait of a Coast Resort* (Newport: Lincoln County Historical Society, 1975), 16.

7. Compiler unknown, "Yaquina Bay Oregon Jetties at Entrance," extracts from *U.S. Army Corps of Engineers Reports*, 1966, OCHC #86.127.9.

8. "$200 Bid for Jail," *News-Times,* undated, 1982.

9. Ibid.

10 Price, 18.

11. Ben W. Olcott, comp., *Oregon Blue Book* (Salem: State Printing Department, 1915), 157.

LIFESTYLES OF THE EARLY NEWPORTERS

Chickens running the sandy streets, no electricity, no indoor plumbing, and candlelit rooms were just some of the inconveniences tourists and residents alike experienced in early-day Newport. Several sources in the archives at the Oregon Coast History Center offer some insights into the lifestyles of early-day Newporters.

Newport began on the Bayfront in 1866 when Sam Case and his associate, Dr. James R. Bayley, constructed the Ocean House Hotel on the bluff now occupied by the Yaquina Bay Coast Guard Station. The Ocean House was the first resort hotel on the Oregon Coast and the nucleus of the settlement which became known as Newport.[1] With eight acres, the Ocean House was a favorite place among children because it offered the only yard in town[2] and was a good place to pitch a tent and camp.[3]

Case wrote this idyllic description of Newport life:

The beach is within a stone's throw of the hotels; in fact, it is directly in front of the Ocean House, which is designated especially for the entertainment of the seaside

Front Street (now called the Bayfront) in Newport in 1895.

visitor, and occupies an elevated shelf overlooking the bay and ocean in a most pleasant situation. Many people find additional pleasure in camping out in the thick growth of small trees that covers the hills, and the great number of romantic and secluded nooks that seem to invite the pleasure seeker to erect his own habitation and enjoy the rustic simplicity of the situation.[4]

The year after Case opened the Ocean House, he got word that a fellow settler, James Craigie, had a house full of daughters. Craigie, a native of Scotland, had helped

construct Fort Boise in 1839 while under the employ of the Hudson's Bay Company. His wife, Mary Ann, was the daughter of a Bannock Indian chief. Case called on the Craigie family in hopes someone would be interested in working at his hotel. Craigie's daughter, Mary, who was known to be a good cook and housekeeper, went to work for Case. The following year Case and Mary Craigie were married.[5]

In January 1886, Case bought out his partner and assumed full ownership of the Ocean House. Case then had to secure furniture for his hotel, because at some point prior, J.M. Rader, who had been in charge of the hotel operations, lost the furniture to a creditor. Case purchased the furniture back "for about half what it was actually worth."[6]

The Ocean House was by no means Case's only business venture; he owned much of the land that makes up the Bayfront today. In the 1880s, Case was selling Bayfront lots for $100 each.[7] Case also served as Newport's postmaster.[8] Apparently the post office was the center of social activity; in 1877, a Newport vacationer wrote, "The people seem to do little but await the mail and then gossip and speculate on the news received from the valley."[9] The

Mary Case in her later years. Daughter of James and Mary Ann Craigie, Mary went to work for Sam Case as a cook and housekeeper at the Ocean House in 1867. They were married a year later.

visitor added Newport was "a city in imagination, since there are but a few old dwellings built in the sand on the shore of Yaquina Bay."[10]

Perhaps in an effort to build up activity, Case persuaded his nephew, Alonzo, to move his family to Newport. Alonzo operated a general store,[11] and his son, Arthur, drove a wagon that carried guests and freight to the Ocean House.[12]

Tourists had three choices when it came to accommodations: the Ocean House Hotel, the Bay View, or tenting. Permanent residents lived in the hotels, saloons, or stores they operated; a few enjoyed a separate home or farm of their own. Two or three boarding units were available at the Briggs House. In the summer, these were rented out to campers, in the winter to "the poorer drifting class of movers." These drifters "came and went . . . as did the seaweed on the shore, thrown there by a flood tide, only to be drawn away by the next ebb."[13]

One of the few accounts of early-day Newport life was written by Lucy F. Blue. In 1873, Lucy, then

The Bay View House (hotel) after the turn of the century.

eight years old, traveled to Newport with her parents, Mr. and Mrs. George Stevens. They had made arrangements to lease the Ocean House from Case for the summer. The Stevenses traveled from Corvallis from early morning to dusk in a four-horse wagon which stopped at noon to change horses. After spending the night in Elk City, they rode the mail boat for the last twenty-five miles of their adventure down the Yaquina River to Newport. There was no road from Elk City to Newport at this time.

Her account of what she saw when she got off the boat illustrates Newport's humble beginnings. They landed at a "rickety wharf" in front of the Bay View, which was run by Peter and Cerena Abbey. Next to the Abbey wharf was a sand beach with weathered logs "strewn aimlessly

The Davis-Copeland family camping at the foot of Fall Street, ca. 1900.

Newport's first wharf, built by A.W. Wright in the 1870s. This may have been the "rickety wharf" referred to by Lucy Blue. (David Stryker)

about" with one or two removed to make a path to the stores and saloons. Next to the beach was another wharf "rather out of repair," a small general store owned by Fred Sawtelle, and a saloon operated by his brother. Across the street was the Bay View, a saloon, some shacks ("not fit to live in"), and a large double building that was a store and a saloon. Upstairs were living rooms and a hall. The hall, the recreation center of the time, was used "for church services of whatever denomination the minister of the gospel happened to be who had wandered that way." Most frequently it was used as a dance hall.[14]

The Stevenses were responsible for providing the Ocean House guests with meals. In the 1870s, both the Ocean House and the Bay View charged lodgers eight dollars a week, including meals.[15] Frequently the Stevenses purchased fish for their guests from the local Siletz Indians for ten cents a pound. Sometimes Lucy's father would row a boat out in front of the hotel and catch the day's supply of fish. Crabs were caught by snagging them with a large hook on the end of a stiff pole. A butcher shop was unheard of; meat was purchased from neighbors who, when they planned to slaughter a cow, pig, or sheep, would go door to door and take orders for the surplus meat. Almost everyone in town had his or her own chickens.

Other supplies came with the arrival of J.J. Winant's boat, which ran back and forth between Newport and San Francisco. When Winant left Newport, his boat was loaded with Yaquina Bay oysters and/or lumber. Lucy remembered with fondness that when "Captain Jimmy" returned with supplies, he frequently treated the children of Newport to bananas or oranges from the big city.[16]

At this time, crossing the Yaquina Bay bar to the ocean was risky business. There were no jetties or even a tugboat to tow sailboats in and out of the bay. In the 1870s, at least three vessels (the *John Hunter*, the *Lizzie*, and the

The Ocean House was a favorite site among children because it offered the only yard in town.

29

Caroline Medeau) were destroyed when they ended up aground on South Beach. Both the *Lizzie* and the *Caroline Medeau* were leaving the harbor when the wind lulled and the waves forced the powerless vessels ashore. Both vessels were bound for San Francisco loaded with oysters from Oysterville and lumber from the sawmill at Oneatta.[17]

English author and world traveler Wallis Nash visited Newport in the 1870s and provided a few more insights into the "infant" settlement. Nash wrote of going to a store next to the Abbey Hotel that was operated by Butch Hammond to chat and smoke. The place was lit by a single smoking wall lamp. As Nash and his companions chatted, local Siletz Indians brought in a dead sea otter to sell to the proprietor. The bidding went into the hundreds of dollars as the sea otter was considered all but extinct at that time.[18]

Nash also wrote of attending a dance held in the large hall mentioned by Lucy Blue. He described it as

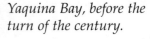

Yaquina Bay, before the turn of the century.

"about fifty feet long, and seventy-five feet wide and lighted with candles in tin sconces. Wreaths of green and flowers were hung on the walls for the occasion. At the far end there was a platform, and on it the musicians were sitting — a harp, fiddle, and cornet." Nash was amazed that in this town of "two or three houses" there were "thirty couples in the room, besides a row of wallflowers young and old." Nash concluded that most of them were visitors camped in tents along the bay. Nash and three or four "Indian men" found amusement in the "occasional entanglements some of the dancers got into in spite of the word of command of the conductor."[19]

Nash wrote that during the "camping-out months," dances were held at the hall once or twice a week. The invitations were general and admission was by contribution to pay for the band and the candles. Nash also mentioned the tourist accommodations of the day: "We passed several camps of holiday makers, their white tents planted among the bushes and cliffs, with little broken ravines giving access for each camp to the sandy beach below."[20]

L.A. Dennick wrote an account of his travels to the Yaquina Bay area that appeared in an 1877 edition of the *Corvallis Gazette* newspaper. He wrote, "nearly all the campers go over to South Beach." Instead of South Beach, Dennick chose to camp in the Nye Beach area. When the rain refused to stop, Dennick spent the night in the home of acquaintances John Nye and family. Their home was located approximately at the intersection of today's Third and

Brook streets. When the rain finally died down, he set up camp on the "Nye Ranch."[21]

In the decade that followed, tremendous changes took place in this primitive town of campers: the railroad arrived in Lincoln County, the Yaquina Bay was dredged, and the government began construction of a jetty. Large ocean-going ships and passenger vessels could then enter Yaquina Bay with a measure of safety. The pleasure-seekers Case wrote about began to flock to Newport by the trainload. Case and Bayley formally platted and named their town and expanded the Ocean House. During the 1880s, land values increased along with the population of Newport, which shot up 330 percent.[22] However, a letter in the archives at the Oregon Coast History Center, written by Newport resident Lucius Phelps on April 20, 1870, indicates that some things had not changed: "The

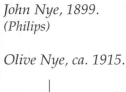

John Nye, 1899.
(Philips)

Olive Nye, ca. 1915.

winter just past has been a rather stormy one here in Oregon . . . the storms being rain." Phelps added, "We have had a good deal of windy weather."[23]

END NOTES

1. Richard L. Price, *Newport, Oregon 1866-1936: Portrait of a Coast Resort* (Newport: Lincoln County Historical Society, 1975), 07.
2. Lucy F. Blue, *A Glimpse of Newport 75 Years Ago* (Waldport: Mr. and Mrs. Paul Van De Velde, 1949), 02.
3. L.A. Dennick, "To Newport and Back," *Corvallis Gazette*, 17 Aug. 1877.
4. Sam Case, "Yaquina Bay, Oregon," *The Westshore Magazine*, vol. 15, 1889.
5. Fred Lockley, "Impressions and Observations of the Journal Man: Interview with Mary Case," *Oregon Journal*, 11 June 1923.
6. "Property Transfer," *Corvallis Gazette*, 29 Jan. 1886.
7. Case, warranty deed, lots two and three, block thirteen, 17 May 1884, Oregon Coast History Center Research Library, Newport.
8. "Yaquina Bay As Resort," *Corvallis Gazette*, 04 Aug. 1876.
9. Dennick.
10. Ibid.
11. "Former Newport Citizen Dies in Oak Harbor, Washington," *Yaquina Bay News*, 19 Feb. 1920.
12. "Descendants To Visit Here," *News-Times*, 14 Oct. 1982.
13. Blue, 03.
14. Ibid., 02.
15. "Yaquina Bay As Resort."
16. Blue, 02-04.
17. "Wreck of the Schr. *Lizzie*," *Corvallis Gazette*, 25 Feb. 1875. "Another Vessel Ashore," *Corvallis Gazette*, 14 April 1876.
18. Wallis Nash, *A Lawyer's Life On Two Continents* (Boston: The Gorham Press, 1919), 146.
19. Nash, *Oregon: There and Back in 1877* (London : MacMillan and Co., 1878; Corvallis: Oregon State University Press, 1976), 155.
20. Ibid., 150-151.
21. Dennick.
22. Price, 17.
23. Lucius W. Phelps to Abigail P. Dodge, 20 April 1870, Oregon Coast History Center Research Library, Newport.

THE WRECK OF THE *YAQUINAS*

THE END OF A STEAM DREAM

Prosperity built on steam — ships and trains moving freight and passengers — was the American dream of the 1800s. In 1872, this dream rolled into town. Colonel Thomas Egenton Hogg arrived in Corvallis from New York and set out to sell the people of Benton County (which then included Lincoln County) his version of the steam dream. He promoted a transportation empire in which passengers and freight could move with relative ease by rail from Corvallis to Yaquina Bay, where they could then transfer to San Francisco-bound ships. Hogg's railroad also would carry tourists on excursions to the coast. His plans included a steamship line running on the Willamette River that would connect Corvallis with Portland and a railroad line east that would connect with the transcontinental railroad. Hogg claimed he knew the right "moneyed" people and could make it all happen. His dream, however, would draw to a close with a recurring nightmare: the wreck of two ships called *Yaquina*.

Above: 1910 first-class, round-trip ferry ticket from Newport to Yaquina issued by Southern Pacific Railroad, formerly Hogg's Oregon Pacific Railroad.

Opposite: The wreck of the Yaquina Bay *at the south jetty, December 1888.*

Train at Yaquina City, ca. 1900. Many thought Yaquina City, six miles east of Newport, would become another San Francisco.

The realization of Hogg's dream required money — money he did not have. It took years of selling bonds to his non-existent Willamette Valley and Coast Railway Company before a train whistle would be heard on Yaquina Bay. Hogg also secured a twenty-year tax exemption and free tidelands from the Oregon Legislature. Even with this windfall, he still needed more capital. Hogg began selling bonds to locals and back East. After many setbacks and a false start, construction of a standard-gauge railroad began in September 1881, nearly 10 years after Hogg started promoting his dream. Not until March 1885 did the first train run from Corvallis to Yaquina Bay.[1]

A train trip to the coast in the 1880s was not as easy as one might think. An account appearing in a July 1885 edition of the *Corvallis Weekly Gazette* documents the hard-

ships passengers endured on one particular ride. The seventy passengers rode on open cars. Between Corvallis and Philomath, vegetation had grown so thick over the tracks that it nearly brought the locomotive dubbed *Corvallis* to a halt. After making it past Summit, the train was forced to stop at a tunnel under repair after a fire. The passengers were obliged to walk around the hill where a second train was waiting for them.

The reporter remarked upon reaching their destination, "At Yaquina City on the arrival of the train, the band discoursed fine music, and amid the noise and confusion, the whistling of opposition boats, and the sight of the ocean steamer *Yaquina*, one might easily imagine himself on the

End of the line at Yaquina City, 1880s. Repair shops are pictured at left, the roundhouse at center.

San Francisco docks." The return trip was without incident until they got over the coast range. A hot sun caused the railroad tracks to expand and spread apart. To prevent derailment, the train was forced to stop on several occasions while workers realigned the track. The return trip from Newport to Corvallis took eleven-and-a-half hours.[2]

The mention by the reporter of San Francisco seems like an exaggeration, but it was probably no accident. Many believed Yaquina City (where Sawyer's Landing is today) would become an important shipping terminus not unlike San Francisco. The ocean-going steamer *Yaquina*, later renamed *Yaquina City*, was the flagship of the railroad. This 231-foot steamer offered a direct connection to San Francisco. On its first experimental trip, the *Yaquina City* carried 300 tons of Willamette Valley wheat.[3] Hogg's line quickly won the favor of Willamette Valley farmers; he beat the shipping rates of his Portland competition by about 27 percent. On return trips from San Francisco, the *Yaquina City* carried freight destined for towns from Roseburg to Amity.[4] Hogg's line acted like a Federal Express of its day. The speed of Hogg's delivery was demonstrated when six railroad cars of freight were unloaded from the *Yaquina City* on a Saturday evening, shipped by rail to Corvallis, and then by steamship to Albany. By Monday the freight was loaded on railroad cars ready for shipment to southern Oregon.[5] Traveling salesmen found that customers in the Willamette Valley and southern Oregon were requesting orders be shipped via the *Yaquina* route as it was cheaper

The SS Yaquina City *at the Oregon Pacific Railroad dock, ca. 1886.*

and faster than the normal route through Portland.[6]

By 1886, trains were running to Yaquina Bay on a daily basis. The combination of freight and tourist travel led to an unprecedented increase in economic activity. Observing the growth, a reporter wrote, "Yaquina City, however, is destined we believe to become the metropolis of Oregon. Here is where the railroad terminus is and here is where the docks are located, here is where substantial improvements are going on and here is where everything indicates progress, push, and population."[7] In addition to improvements at Yaquina City, construction of the south jetty was well under way. Completion of this project would make it easier for ocean-going vessels to get in and out of the bay. In Newport, the Ocean House and Bayview House hotels were added onto and remodeled. Several new buildings and residences also sprung up in Newport as well as a hotel at South Beach.[8] When rumors spread of the spur line extending south of Yaquina Bay, developers hastily drew plats and began selling lots to non-existent towns such as Highland, For Far, and Seal Rocks.

On the surface, Hogg's railroad, by then renamed the Oregon Pacific Railroad, seemed to be prospering; but things were far from perfect. A lack of capital or mismanagement may have contributed to a series of unfortunate accidents. Hogg spent much of his time back East or in San Francisco entertaining potential

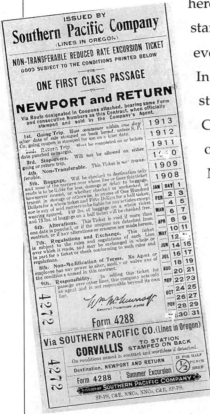

investors. The first tragedy occurred in 1885 when a locomotive ran into a open flatcar loaded with passengers, throwing everyone off. A six-year-old girl was killed and several others injured.[9] On October 30, 1886, the railway experienced two train wrecks. A train of twenty-three cars headed to Yaquina derailed just below Nashville. When news of the wreck was telegraphed to Yaquina, a train with a salvage crew was dispatched to the scene. This train met with a rock slide and was thrown off the tracks. Two men were killed and three were seriously injured.[10] That same month, a sailor fell overboard the *Yaquina City* and drowned.[11] A few weeks later, a well-known Polk County physician was killed when he fell down a loading chute for the *Yaquina City*.[12] Local newspapers accused the railway of gross negligence for leaving the hatchway chute open at night.[13]

The misfortunes of the Oregon Pacific Railroad then switched to the seas. On December 5, 1887, its steamship *Yaquina City* went aground while entering the Yaquina Bay. One of the chains connecting the rudder to the steering wheel broke and became entangled with the drive screw, causing the engine to stop. The ship was then washed up on South Beach. The passengers waded to the beach and their freight was unloaded without incident. For awhile it looked as if the *Yaquina City* would be

Below: Token from Brunks Billiard Hall. Reverse side reads, "Monogram Cigar Store, good for 10¢ in trade, Yaquina, OR."

Opposite: First-class round-trip passage aboard the Southern Pacific Railroad, 1910.

refloated and on her way, but it was not to be.[14] A few weeks after it was grounded, the *Yaquina City* was sold to a salvager for $9,100. This sale was said to be a bargain, as the steamer was equipped with two $12,000 boilers in good condition and a fairly new $9,000 drive shaft.[15] It is not known whether the boilers were salvaged. Several reliable eyewitness accounts report the *Yaquina City* eventually broke up.[16]

Jack Fogarty, who was then a lad of ten living at South Beach, recalled that onlookers gathered as the steamer washed ashore and a bonfire was built to warm the wet passengers. He also remembered locals salvaging the furniture and freight left on board — the most prized find being kegs of liquor.[17] When a reporter from Corvallis visited a few months after the wreck, he noted, "a number of persons have relics of the Yaquina on their mantle boards and center tables."[18]

Immediately after the loss of the *Yaquina City*, the line began searching for a replacement vessel. By March 1888, Hogg had chartered the steamer *City of Topeka* for his line.[19] The *City of Topeka* made the trip from Baltimore to San Francisco in fifty-three days. Hogg renamed the steamer *Yaquina Bay*. Many secondary accounts report the steamer wrecked on its first attempt to enter Yaquina Bay. However, two newspaper accounts indicate in July 1888 the *Yaquina Bay* made a trip from Yaquina City to San Francisco.[20] Loaded with freight and a delegation of educators bound for the National Teacher's Convention in San

Francisco, the trip was made in just over thirty hours.[21]

In December 1888, the *Yaquina Bay* went aground against the south jetty of its namesake bay. The exact circumstances of the ship's demise are unclear. No local newspaper accounts of the day are in existence. But one thing is for certain: the captain in charge of the vessel, William Kelly Jr., was fired by the line and had his license revoked on charges of gross negligence.[22] The *Yaquina Bay* broke up and sank.

The wreck of the two *Yaquinas* marked the beginning of the end of Hogg's steam dream. Lloyd Palmer, in his book on railroading in Lincoln County, *Steam Towards the Sunset*, summed it up: "These two accidents frightened

Wreck of the SS Yaquina City *at South Beach, December 1887.*

43

many of the potential investors away, and it became increasingly difficult for Hogg to secure money for his rail-road."[23] The line went into receivership and was placed on the auction block. Much of the line built by Hogg remains in use, transporting freight for Toledo's Georgia-Pacific kraft paper mill. The rail line now ends at the Toledo mill. For perhaps a year, the transportation network envisioned by Hogg was nearly realized. Mismanagement, bad luck, and a lack of capital, followed by the entry into the auto-mobile age, prevented the steam dream from materializing again.

END NOTES
1. Lloyd Palmer, *Steam Towards the Sunset* (Newport: Lincoln County Historical Society, 1990), 6.
2. "The O.P. Excursion," *Corvallis Weekly Gazette*, 10 July 1885.
3. "Steamship *Yaquina*," *Corvallis Weekly Gazette*, 11 Sept. 1885.
4. "The S.S. *Yaquina*," *Corvallis Weekly Gazette*, 26 Feb. 1886.
5. "Quick Work," *Corvallis Weekly Gazette*, 19 Mar. 1886.

Train from Toledo on its way to Yaquina City, ca. 1900.

6. "Goods Sent via *Yaquina*," *Corvallis Weekly Gazette*, 21 May 1886.

7. Mat Purphy, "Corvallis to Yaquina Bay," *Corvallis Weekly Gazette*, 25 Jun. 1886.

8. Ibid.

9. "Railroad Accident," *Corvallis Weekly Gazette*, 04 Sept. 1885.

10. "Railroad Disaster," *Corvallis Weekly Gazette*, 05 Nov. 1886.

11. "Sailor Drowned," *Corvallis Weekly Gazette*, 19 Nov. 1886.

12. "Fatal Accident," *Corvallis Weekly Gazette*, 3 Dec. 1886.

13. "Report Vs. Facts," *Corvallis Weekly Gazette*, 10 Dec. 1886.

14. "Steamer Aground," *Corvallis Weekly Gazette*, 09 Dec. 1887.

15. "Disposed Of," *Corvallis Weekly Gazette*, 30 Dec. 1887.

16. *Pacific Spruce Corporation and its Subsidiaries*, ed. Bolling Arthur Johnson (Newport: C.D. Johnson Co., 1924, Lincoln County Historical Society, 1996), 21.

17. Jack Fogarty, "Ocean Claims Steamship *Yaquina City*," *Newport News*, 09 Sept. 1965.

18. "A Trip to the Bay," *Corvallis Weekly Gazette*, 17 Feb. 1888.

19. "It is reported...," *Corvallis Weekly Gazette*, 16 Mar. 1888.

20. "Col. T. Egenton Hogg...," *Corvallis Weekly Gazette*, 11 Jan. 1889.

21. Ibid.

22. *Pacific Spruce Corporation*, 21-22.

23. Palmer, 10.

Oregon Pacific Railroad docks and terminal at Yaquina City, 1883.

CITIZEN JONES
AND THE CREATION OF A COUNTY

"Lincoln County's most distinguished and progressive citizen," proclaimed a newspaper article describing Benjamin Franklin Jones shortly after his death in 1925. His funeral services were held in Newport and his burial in Toledo, a fitting arrangement since Jones shaped the development of both these communities. In fact, Lincoln County may very well owe its existence to the political fortitude of Ben Jones.

Jones led Lincoln County's secession from Benton County and was its first clerk. He also served at various times as the mayor of Newport and Toledo. He platted the community of Otter Rock and was its first significant developer. And, while serving in the Oregon Legislature, he introduced a bill that would lead to construction of the Oregon Coast Highway and change the economy of this area forever.

Ben Jones was born in 1858 into a large, closely knit Kansas family. He was the firstborn of Wilson Lee Jones and Rebecca Graham Jones. Rebecca came from a very large family headed by brothers William and John Graham.

Opposite: Benjamin Franklin Jones: steamboat captain, lawyer, mayor, legislator, developer, and father of Lincoln County.

47

Ben Jones as Oregon legislator, 1907.

Wilson Jones and his family lived near the Grahams in Prairie City, Kansas. The two families had become close friends; with the marriage of Wilson Lee and Rebecca, they became kin. The rich soil and favorable climate enabled both families to enjoy a measure of prosperity.

The families' good fortune began to wane as the slavery controversy came to a boil. Two cities near Prairie City were sacked by a pro-slavery group known as the Bushwhackers. Fortunately, an attack on Prairie City was averted with the arrest of the Bushwhackers.

After the Civil War broke out in 1861, the families' crops suffered when their young men who worked the fields went off to war. An invasion of pests ravaged what few crops remained. The families found themselves shunned by some relatives because they supported the Union (anti-slavery) cause.

In 1864, the John Graham and Dr. William Graham families decided they had had enough of war-torn Kansas and headed West to start a new life in Oregon. They left Kansas with two covered wagons (one was of use for four miles), eighty head of cattle, several saddle horses, and carriages. After a stopover in eastern Oregon, they headed to Corvallis, where the Dr. William Graham family remained. His brother continued westward to what was then known as the "Yaquina Strip," an area along the Yaquina Bay that was removed from the Siletz Indian Reservation in 1866 and opened for settlement.[1] John Graham took out a 160-acre land claim on what became the city of Toledo,[2] and he is regarded as the town's founder.

While his relatives started their new life in Oregon, twelve-year-old Ben Jones remained in Prairie City with his parents and his siblings, Wiley, Mary, Joseph, John, and Thomas. Ben's father probably was unable to travel West because he was suffering from injuries incurred while fighting for the Union in the Civil War. Wilson Jones never recovered from his wounds and died in 1866 at age thirty-two.[3] A year later, the Joneses lost their once-thriving flour mill and farm to back taxes. After Wilson's death and the loss of the farm, John Graham sent his brother Joseph to Kansas to escort Rebecca and her children to Toledo via the transcontinental railroad. Rebecca arrived in Toledo in 1870 with all her children except for Wiley, Wilson's child from a previous marriage, who stayed in Kansas. When Rebecca arrived in Toledo, relatives found her depressed from the death of her husband, impoverished, and in poor health. Four years later, Rebecca died after contracting pneumonia.[4]

Rebecca's children were then taken in by various

The Ben Jones family, 1910-1911. Standing, left to right: Ben Jones's wife, Ella; son Vinton; daughter-in-law Oneatta; sons Vernon, Francis, and Everett; and Ben Jones. Sitting in front, left to right: Julia and Ralph, children of Everett and Oneatta; and Gladys, Ben's daughter. Sitting above the trio is Ben's daughter, Nell.

members of the Graham family. Ben Jones, at age sixteen, continued his education at the Oregon Agricultural College (now Oregon State University). After two years of college, Jones took a job in the lumber industry, then as a mail carrier on horseback (and sometimes afoot) between Elk City and Corvallis.[5] His experience at carrying the mail on the muddy roads of Lincoln County made him an early advocate for road improvements.[6] Jones then married Ella Miller in 1881 and moved to Astoria, where he engaged in "boating and freighting" on the Columbia River. The Jones family returned in 1883 to Toledo, where Jones ran a steamboat on Yaquina Bay until 1892.[7] His last stint at steamboating was working for the government in the construction of the

Yaquina Bay jetties.[8]

His role as an advocate for Lincoln County began when his steamboating career ended. At age thirty-five, Jones led a delegation from the central Oregon Coast to the county seat of Corvallis, seeking 3,000 feet of lumber for road improvements. Jones acted as the group's speaker and presented its case before the county court. Jones was jokingly told by the county officials that the people on the coast were a "bunch of clam diggers" and did not need any roads. Jones replied, "With the cooperation of the balance of the clam diggers, we are going to create a new county."[9]

When the delegation members returned home, they began working for the formation of a new coastal county; Jones was one of their most tireless lobbyists, writing and circulating the needed petitions. Jones, Lee Wade, and Senator Charles Crosno worked together, lobbying for the formation of what was originally to be called Bay County.

Many people in Benton County took their efforts as a joke; others told Jones they were glad to lose the western part of their county because that's where all the criminals and paupers lived. At this time, there were efforts by others to form new counties in eastern Oregon that were unsuccessful. Crosno later told Jones that if the two of them had not been hunting-partners with several key members of the legislature, Lincoln County probably never would have materialized. When the bill for the new county came up for a vote, the name Bay County was changed to Lincoln County by Oregon Senator Cogswell, a Civil War veteran and admirer of Abraham Lincoln. Ben Jones was appointed by Governor Pennoyer as Lincoln County's first clerk.[10]

Jones also served as mayor of Lincoln County's seat, Toledo, from 1896 to 1900. He continued his education at this time, graduating with a law degree from Oregon Agricultural College. He was admitted to the Oregon Bar in 1897. The following year he resigned his clerk position and began practicing law in Toledo.[11] Jones valued education and came very close to making Newport a college town. In the 1903 legislative session, he introduced a bill to establish a Normal School (teacher's college) in Newport. After passing the house and senate, it was vetoed by Governor Chamberlain. Jones secured the needed two-thirds vote to override the veto, but the vote fell short when one of his key supporters was absent the day of the vote.[12]

Jones's other legislative accomplishments are impressive. In 1907, he introduced a bill that became law calling for parent-teacher meetings in Oregon schools. In that same session, he introduced a bill giving women the right to vote, but it was defeated. Transportation was his greatest legislative concern. He introduced a bill to regulate railroad rates and another, which passed, to fund the operation of the locks on Willamette River at no cost to shippers.

He also championed transportation as a private citizen and lawyer. In 1907, Jones successfully filed suit against the Southern Pacific Company compelling it to

return passenger service between Albany and Yaquina City. The archives of the Oregon Coast History Center contain a complaint Jones authored for presentation before the railroad commission accusing the Corvallis and Eastern Railroad Company of overselling passenger tickets and exceeding freight capacities, resulting in inhuman and life-threatening conditions for both people and livestock.[13] In 1908, Jones filed suits against the Wells Fargo Express Company and the Pacific Express Company alleging their rates unjust. As a result of Jones's efforts, express rates in Oregon were reduced twenty-five percent. Jones also served on the Port of Newport and lobbied the federal government for dredging Yaquina Bay and for jetty improvements.[14]

Despite these many victories, political defeat came to Jones while living in Roseburg and working as the reg-

Ben Jones's law office in Toledo, probably 1908. From right are Ben Jones and daughters Nell and Gladys.

istrar at the United States Land Office processing land claims. He was defeated by W.C. Hawley in the primary election for the U.S. House of Representatives. Jones attributed the loss to the politically active prohibitionist.[15]

While his political career was certainly the most headline-capturing aspect of the Ben Jones story, it was just one part of Jones's varied life. He was also a family man and real estate developer. In 1907, he purchased much of the land that makes up present-day Otter Rock and platted the town. He was Otter Rock's first important developer. Jones named some of the streets after his wife, Gabriella (Ella), and two girls, Gladys and Leone Nell. Ben and Ella Jones also had four sons: Vinton, Vernon, Francis, and

Highway near Otter Rock, late 1920s.

Everett. Each summer the Ben Jones family and his sister's family, the Hornings, would camp at Otter Rock. In 1908, when lumber from the steamer *Minnie Kelton* washed ashore at Otter Rock, the two families built several cottages and a hotel from the bounty. While the hotel is long gone, the cottage built for Ben Jones still stands. By 1912, with the lumber from the *Kelton* exhausted, Ben Jones and some investors built a sawmill in Otter Rock. In 1918, Jones turned the sawmill over to the U.S. Army's Spruce Division to help with the war effort.[16]

OTTER ROCK HOTEL AT OTTER POINT NEAR NEWPORT ORE.

Hotel at Otter Rock, ca. 1912. Ben Jones's cottage is visible just behind the hotel.

It was about this time he returned to public office after being elected to the Oregon House of Representatives. In 1919, Jones wrote the bill that would put the Oregon Coast on the (highway) map. His legislation authorized the construction of the Roosevelt Coast Military Highway along the coast from the Columbia River to the California line. The United States government was to pay for half of the construction costs; the other half was to be funded by bonds issued by the State of Oregon.[17]

With no opposition in the Senate, the $2.5 million bonding enactment for the Jones proposal passed.[18] It then went before Oregon voters, who gave it their approval by a wide margin.[19] Someone once nicknamed it "Ben Jones's Wagon Road," but today we know it as Highway 101. While approval came quickly from Oregon lawmakers and voters, funding from the federal government took longer.

Construction of the Ben Jones Bridge, 1927.
(Oregon Department of Transportation)

But by 1923, construction of the highway was well under way in northern Lincoln County and southern Tillamook County. Jones, who at age sixty-four had just the year before completed a term as Newport's mayor, traveled up north to view the tangible results of his legislative efforts. He reported back to the local paper that the contractor was doing splendid work on the highway.[20]

Jones did not live to see the completion of his greatest legislative legacy. He died of heart failure at his home while on his lunch break from his Newport law office in March 1925. Two years later, a bridge over Rocky Creek at the north end of the Otter Rock Loop was named after Ben Jones for his efforts at making the Oregon Coast Highway a reality.

END NOTES
1. Dr. Benjamin Graham Horning, "Comments Concerning the Genealogy of Mary Jones Horning," 1984, typed manuscript, Oregon Coast History Center clipping file.
2. David D. Fagan, *History of Benton County, Oregon* (Portland: A. G. Walling, Printer, 1885), 514.
3. Horning.
4. Ibid.
5. Chapman Publishing Co. eds., *Portrait and Biographical Record of Western Oregon* (Chicago: Chapman Publishing Co., 1904), 725.
6. Mrs. Dorry Smith, "Ben Jones' Wagon Road," letter to the edi-

tor, unidentified newspaper article, ca. 1936.

7. Chapman Publishing, 725.
8. "Hon. B.F. Jones," *Yaquina Bay News*, Winter 1918.
9. "The Passing of B.F. Jones," *Lincoln County Leader*, March 1925.
10. Ben F. Jones, "What Hounds and 3,000 feet of Lumber Had to Do With the Formation of Lincoln County," *Yaquina Bay News*, March 1923.
11. Chapman Publishing Co., 725.
12. "Hon. B. F. Jones."
13. Ben F. Jones, "Before the Railroad Commission of Oregon, B.F. Jones Vs. Corvallis and Eastern Railroad Company," 1907.
14. Ibid.
15. "Drys Blamed for Defeat," unidentified newspaper, Oregon Coast History Center "Jones" biography clipping file.
16. Steve M. Wyatt, editor, *Pictorial History of Otter Rock*, (Newport: Lincoln County Historical Society, 1996), 22-42.
17. "Roosevelt Highway Proposed by B.F. Jones," *Yaquina Bay News*, 23 Jan. 1919.
18. "Roosevelt Military Highway Bill Passed," *Yaquina Bay News*, 27 Feb. 1919.
19. "Roosevelt Highway Carries," *Yaquina Bay News*, 5 June 1919.
20. "Roosevelt Highway Work is Making Good Progress," *Yaquina Bay News*, 26 July 1923.

Dedication of the Ben Jones Bridge, September 17, 1927. (Oregon Department of Transportation)

Outpost Alsea
Early-Day Settlement on the Bay

In the 1870s, a handful of settlers with "pluck and muscle" and "a little cash capital" put down roots along the Alsea Bay.[1] They had a great deal of hope for better days ahead. Believers in the Alsea were certain that after the railroad came to the Yaquina Bay and harbor improvements were made, prosperity would trickle their way. As one eloquent Alsea settler put it, "The sun shines alike on the just and unjust, and my dear Christian friends, when the sun of prosperity is made to shine on your inland valleys and hills, our verdant earth around the beautiful Alsea Bay will bud and bloom like the rose of Sharon . . ."[2]

No one would argue the early settlers needed pluck, muscle, and money. The Alsea Bay, Yachats, and what is now south Lincoln County were removed from the outside world. Alsea's connection to Corvallis, then the county seat, was a single road over the coast range that became impassible as soon as the rains began each fall. The best road to the area was the beach between Alsea and Newport, though access often was threatened by storms and high tides. Since the Alsea Bay had not been thorough-

Opposite: Pack train, probably south Lincoln County, 1910s. Though the economy in the Alsea Bay area improved by the turn of the century, transportation remained primitive until major road improvements in the 1920s and '30s.

59

ly surveyed, access to ocean-going boats was uncertain; it was unclear whether the bay was deep enough to accommodate shipping traffic.[3] Because of the area's isolation, the sun of prosperity took a good while to shine on the settlers of Alsea.

The Alsea Bay and all of what is now Lincoln County were first put on the map with the creation of the Siletz Indian Reservation in 1855. The Siletz Reservation, which was twenty miles wide and stretched from Tillamook County into present-day Lane County, was closed to Euro-American settlement. The reservation's acreage began to shrink when the government purchased the land around Yaquina Bay to the north bank of the Alsea Bay. The government gave what it considered the four main tribes of the reservation (Coos, Siuslaw, Umpqua, and Alsea) $16,500 in compensation. In the last few days of 1865, this land, now central Lincoln County, was opened for settlement.[4] Meanwhile, lands north of Yaquina Head

and south of the Alsea Bay remained a part of the reservation and closed to settlers. Ten years later, the land south of the Alsea Bay, called the Alsea Sub-Agency, was quietly "abolished"

from the reservation and thrown open for settlement.[5]

As a boy, Charles L. Litchfield (1867-1950) witnessed the last days of the Alsea Sub-Agency and the beginnings of south Lincoln County settlement. In 1873, Litchfield moved with his family to the sub-agency's headquarters, a dilapidated house near present-day Yachats Cemetery. His father, George Litchfield, was appointed to fill the vacancy created by the departure of the previous agent, Sam Case. Charles Litchfield recalled there was a Euro-American community on the north side of the Alsea Bay called Bayview that was more commonly referred to as "White Town." On the south side was a settlement called "Indian Town." The Native American inhabitants of Indian Town lived in government-constructed "shacks." Several white settlers lived adjacent to Indian Town in present-day

Above: Government Hill on the Siletz Indian Reservation, ca. 1900. The Alsea Sub-Agency was removed from the reservation in 1875.

Opposite: The Alsea Sub-Agency headquarters building (in background) at Yachats, 1892.

Newport to Waldport stage run by Lee Doty and Kit Williamson, 1917. The beach was the best road in the Alsea Bay area, though travelers had to be wary of storms and high tides.

Waldport. The non-Indians were ". . . strictly speaking, trespassers and were called squatters. They lived there by permission of the Indian Agent at Yachats."[6]

In April 1875, George Litchfield was ordered to announce the government's abolishment of the Alsea Sub-Agency from the reservation. Indians desiring to remain could do so, providing they could take care of themselves. When the Alsea Sub-Agency closed, most of the 300 Indians relocated. Many ended up returning to their old homes because of the deplorable living conditions on the reservation. The Indians who remained on the Alsea were allowed to stay until 1881, when the government (under pressure) set in motion their removal back to the Siletz reservation.[7]

Five months after the Indians were asked to vacate the first time, settlers began establishing themselves on the Alsea Sub-Agency. When George Litchfield returned to Salem with his family, he informed the press, "Quite a number of squatters are already there, and a number of the more civilized Indians have located claims."[8] A few moved to the area simply to live in seclusion, but the majority of people who put down roots were waiting for the economy to germinate.

In an attempt to attract more people and increase activity on the Alsea, a few settlers submitted glowing accounts of the area's abundant resources to regional newspapers. One of the first appeared in a May 1877 edition of the *Corvallis Gazette*. It described the lower Alsea as a land "covered with a heavy growth of valuable timber" that, once it was cleared of trees, would yield "immense crops of vegetables and grain." The article concluded, "There is room in this valley for a large number of farms, and it is an excellent place for immigrants to find homes." The correspondent admitted the Alsea was "at present distant for market," but countered it was "one of the pleasant and productive spots in Oregon."[9] At this time, the lower Alsea was so remote that despite an abundance of "valuable timber," there was no sawmill. The nearest mill (powered by a waterwheel) was some distance upriver on Mill Creek. When a settler needed lumber, it had to be floated downriver.[10] In short, there were trees everywhere and produce could be grown, but the area lacked a way to mill the logs

Ludeman & McMillan shingle and lumber mill on Mill Creek, 1886. Lumber was floated downriver to settlers on the lower Alsea.

into lumber and customers to sell it to.

Farming and logging were not the only two potential sources of income for settlers on the Alsea Bay: mining also drew fortune-seekers to the area. Early on, there were reports of coal fields in the upper and lower Alsea valleys. The Alsea also experienced a small gold rush that lasted a few years. The "black sand" beaches yielded small quantities of gold when worked. According to one 1877 account, sixty men were working the beaches. Still others were looking inland for gold. While some of the beach mining efforts paid "very well," prospectors might have become ". . . fabulously rich, if some more perfect means of saving fine gold could be successfully employed."[11]

Though the gold rush was less than a financial boom, a glimmer of an economy appeared as the 1870s drew to a close. Funding was obtained for the government to survey the harbor. The schooner *Helen Jane* was built on the bay and put under contract for the survey work.

Homestead sites along the beach and at the bay entrance were surveyed officially. Reports of the land along the "Yahuts" River indicated there were "large bodies of good land . . . enough for a hundred families." In Tidewater, a schoolhouse was opened with fifteen pupils.[12] In 1879, David Ruble left the upper Alsea Valley to purchase the rights to a forty-acre parcel on the lower Alsea for $300 from Lint Starr (for whom Lint Slough is named). Using the stars for lack of a transit, Ruble laid out a new town on this site that came to be named Waldport.[13]

Despite the increased attention, Alsea Bay settlers still felt they were being ignored. In 1880, one settler known as "Beecher" pleaded to readers of the *Corvallis Gazette*, "We want bona fide settlers. We want to see schoolhouses and churches spring up in this part of God's moral heritage. We want roads and something produced to call attention to commerce."[14]

At the time of Beecher's plea, perhaps the most noticeable bastions of civilization on the Alsea were its two

Lint Slough in Waldport, 1910s. This slough was named after Lint Starr, whose forty-acre parcel eventually became the town of Waldport.

Above: The Ruble family, ca. 1890. In 1879, David Ruble settled in the lower Alsea area and, using the stars as his guide, laid out the town of Waldport. Right: The Ruble home in Waldport, ca. 1920.

post offices. One was known as Tidewater, located ten miles up the river at the head of the tide. The second, Collins,[15] was named after George Collins, who carried the mail from Newport. Collins was on the north side of the mouth of the bay[16] about where the north end of the Alsea Bay Bridge is today. In her book, *The Land That Kept its Promise*, Marjorie Hayes wrote the sites and names of the post offices on the Alsea Bay "changed as often as the politics and influences." Names and locations would change sometimes without notification. Some of the lesser-known post offices on the Alsea Bay were Drift Creek, Lutgens, Stanford, Linville, Nice, and Bayview.[17] Once a week the local population gathered at its respective post offices. In 1878, an Alsea Bay settler wrote, "Wednesday noon generally finds about a dozen boats filled with anxious individuals in front of the post office waiting for their papers and news from the outside world. For the time being we almost consider ourselves just a little out of the world but we don't expect to remain so very long."[18]

The weekly trip to the post office remained the most excitement in this "out of the world" place for another four years. In 1882, life began to quicken with the arrival of the first rays of economic prosperity. The economic boom on Yaquina Bay, stimulated by jetty and railroad construction, created a market for vegetables, eggs, butter, and honey from the Alsea Bay area. The demand drove produce prices upward; beef shot up to five cents a pound. The economy of the Alsea Bay was stronger than it ever had been before.[19]

Elmore Cannery boat. The Elmore enterprise owned several canneries on the coast, including a salmon cannery on the Alsea.

Prior to this time, the case could be made that the Alsea Bay had no real economy.

Economic activity increased with the rise of the fishing industry. The first cannery was built on the Alsea in 1886. The needed equipment, along with three Chinese men to run it, came down the beach from Newport on George Collins's freight wagon. Financed by Freeman Dodge and W.W. Harrison, the cannery was set up in the old Lutgens store on the north side of the bay. The first year the partners processed 1,100 cases of salmon. The following year they built a new, larger cannery at what was called Salmon Town (also known as Collins and Collinsville). Reputedly the new cannery processed 5,000 cases of salmon. Like most canneries on the coast at this time, it relied heavily on Chinese labor. This cannery was later sold to the largest cannery on the Columbia River, the Elmore Cannery.[20] The Elmore enterprise controlled a number of canneries up and down the Oregon Coast and in Alaska.[21] Two years after the Elmore takeover, an even larger cannery devoted exclusively to salmon was built on the Alsea Bay. This enterprise was owned and operated by Henry Nice, a long-time fisherman and a former superintendent on the Yaquina Bay jetty construction project. The Nice cannery processed between eight and nine thousand cases of fish a year.[22] Several small, independent canneries also established operations on the bay.[23]

The Alsea fishing industry created a demand for lumber for new buildings and docks. The first mill in Waldport was built by the Baldwin family in 1884. The machinery for this steam-powered operation came from a mill in Toledo. To get the machinery to Waldport, it was floated down the Yaquina River to South Beach and then loaded on a specially made wagon that had four two-foot-wide wheels that were solid tree trunk sections. The boiler was pulled down the beach with five yoke of oxen. This mill became well-known for its box shooks (parts) that were used by the local canneries for shipping. Its boxes were considered some of the best, and it shipped thousands to canneries elsewhere on the coast.[24]

The Barnes store on the north side of the Alsea River at Waldport, early days. This store is a private residence today.

The establishment of an economy brought conclusion to the settlement era on the Alsea. In 1886, newcomers homesteaded or purchased most of the remain-

Mill Street in Waldport, ca. 1912.

ing land parcels.[25] The sawmill and canneries provided products to offer the outside world, and it seemed the "sun of prosperity" finally would be made to shine on the Alsea -- thanks to the pluck, muscle, and cash capital of those early believers.

END NOTES
1. M.J., "From Alsea Bay," *Corvallis Gazette*, 08 March 1878.
2. Beecher, "From Alsea Bay," *Corvallis Gazette*, 26 March 1880.
3. R.A. Bensell, "Alsea Bay and River," *Corvallis Gazette*, 13 Dec. 1878.
4. William Eugene Kent, *The Siletz Reservation 1865-1900* (Newport: Lincoln County Historical Society, 1977), 18.
5. Ibid, 26.
6. Paul and Henrietta R. Van de Velde, *South County and its Early Settlers*, Vol. I, Charles L. Litchfield (Newport: Lincoln County Historical Society), 3-5.
7. E. A. Scwartz, *The Rogue River War and Its Aftermath, 1850 -1980* (Norman: University of Oklahoma Press, 1997), 200-208.

8. "Alsea Reservation Abandoned," *Corvallis Gazette*, 06 Oct. 1876.

9. Rambler, "The Alsea Valley," *Corvallis Gazette*, 04 May 1877.

10. Marjorie H. Hayes, *The Land that Kept Its Promise* (Newport: Lincoln County Historical Society, 1976), 50.

11. "Beach Gold Mining," *Corvallis Gazette*, 28 Nov. 1879.

12. Reporter, "Alsea Bay," *Corvallis Gazette*, 04 July 1879.

13. Hayes, 131.

14. Beecher, "From Alsea Bay," *Corvallis Gazette*, 14 May 1880.

15. Ibid.

16. Beecher, "From Lower Alsea," *Corvallis Gazette*, 13 Feb. 1880.

17. Hayes, 50.

18. M.J., "From Alsea Bay."

19. South Beach, "Alsea Letter," *Corvallis Gazette*, 17 March 1882.

20. Hayes, "Cannery Industry Prospered on Alsea," *News-Times*, 28 May 1970.

21. Chapman Publishing Co. eds., *Portrait and Biographical Record of Western Oregon* (Chicago: Chapman Publishing Co., 1904), 1016.

22. Ibid, 796-797.

23. Hayes, "Cannery Industry."

24. Winifred Morris, "Early Waldport History," unpublished paper in Oregon Coast History Center files, 21 June 1939.

25. Hayes, *The Land that Kept Its Promise*, 64.

Waldport Lumber Company, 1910s.

LINCOLN COUNTY LEGACY
THE RETURNING LITCHFIELDS

Thomas Wolfe said you can't go home again, but several generations of the Litchfield family have proved him wrong. They have left Lincoln County to return again and again. In the process, the Litchfield name has become an important part of this region's history.

The first Litchfield to call Lincoln County home was Gilbert C. In 1857, he left Connecticut for Oregon, traveling to the Grand Ronde Indian Reservation to manage a mercantile there. A few months later, he purchased a store at Siletz. Gilbert wrote his brother, George (grandfather of former Newport attorney G. Kenneth Litchfield), encouraging him to join him in the operation of his thriving store.[1]

Persuaded, George traveled by boat to the Isthmus of Panama, crossed the isthmus by wagon and took another boat to complete the journey to Oregon.[2] Not long after the two brothers were reunited in Siletz, they relocated to Grande Ronde. This was a lucky move, as a massive flood devastated Siletz soon after they left.

Opposite: G. Kenneth Litchfield as a student at Willamette University, about 1929.

73

The George Litchfield family, ca. 1911.

Opposite: George Litchfield, ca. 1870.

In 1863, George met his future wife, Mary A. Craft (1847-1918),[3] at a campsite located where Newport is now. George apparently caught Mary's eye right away. When the party of campers went horseback riding, Mary noticed George was riding a speedy horse and chose a fast horse for herself. The two soon found themselves alone, ahead of the others. Three years later, they met again, this time at the state fair. They married on Christmas day of that year, 1866. The couple first settled down at the Siletz Agency before moving back to Grand Ronde, where they ran a store for many years.[4] In 1872, they sold the store and relocated to Salem, Mary's home-town.[5]

After living in Salem for just a year, they came home again: George had accepted an appointment as the Alsea Indian agent on the Coast Reservation, just north of the Yachats River. George, a master of the various dialects spoken by the Indians at the agency, established its first school. The Litchfields' stay on the reservation was a short one. In 1875, the government closed the reservation and opened the area to settlement. Desiring a good education for their children, the Litchfields returned to Salem.

In 1898, George and Mary's son, Charles, became the next generation of Litchfields to return to Lincoln County. Charles (1867-1950) was employed in the mail service of the Yaquina-Albany railroad line. Charles married Mamie McCluskey (1880-1977), a descendant of a Toledo pioneer family. They settled at Yaquina City, the western end of the railroad line, upriver from Newport (where Sawyer's Landing is now). They later acquired 330 acres of property on Devil's Lake in north Lincoln County. Charles, a hunting and fishing enthusiast, visited the property each summer. It remained in the family into the 1920s.

When Charles was transferred to the Seaside-Portland railroad line in 1913, the Litchfields moved to Portland. Charles remained there until retiring in 1923.[6] Charles and Mamie had four children: John W. (1904-1984), G. Kenneth (born in 1906), Francis (1911-1942), and Charlotte (born in 1916).

G. Kenneth was born in Yaquina City and reared in

Portland. He earned a law degree from Willamette University in 1929. The following year he married another Willamette graduate, Frances McGilvra. Frances first caught his eye years before at the Sunnyside Methodist Church in Portland. It took several years before he gained enough courage to sit with her on Easter Sunday in 1924, and six years more till he married her.

Because of the depressed economy, Kenneth was unable to find employment in the legal profession. So Kenneth and Frances taught school at Bellfountain, Oregon.[7] Kenneth also served as the basketball coach. The team he assembled shortly before leaving Bellfountain went on to win the championship for the entire state in 1937. In those days, high school teams were not divided up by the size of the student body they represented.[8]

Not long before his team was victorious, Kenneth moved his family back to the county of his ancestors.

The Charles Litchfield homestead on Devil's Lake, undated.

Kenneth joined his uncle, George McCluskey, in his Toledo law practice.[9] Kenneth was familiar with his uncle's practice; he had worked for him for at least one summer while he was a student at Willamette University.[10] In 1940, Kenneth and family moved to Newport, where he purchased the practice of Collas L. Marsters for $150.[11] A large oak roll-top desk and safe were included in the deal. Both the desk and safe remained familiar fixtures in Kenneth's office.[12] They are now in the collection of the Oregon Coast History Center.

For most of Kenneth's career, his office was located on Southwest Hurbert across from the Crest Theater (since torn down) between the bowling alley/skating rink and the state-operated liquor store. When he first moved in, his fifteen-dollar monthly rent check was payable to his landlord, Dr. Thurtell. In 1962, Kenneth's office escaped serious damage when the front of the bowling alley next-door was blown off during the infamous Columbus Day storm.[13]

Litchfield brothers Francis, left, and Kenneth on a Newport dock, ca. 1912.

Kenneth Litchfield's Hurbert Street office barely survived the Columbus Day storm of 1962. Next-door the front of the Elks Lodge / bowling alley was blown off. (Roger A. Hart)

Opposite: Kenneth at the Newport Airport, July 20, 1947, during the Miss Newport celebration. Kenneth was instrumental in securing the land for the airport in the 1940s as the city's attorney.

Kenneth practiced law solo for more than thirty years. Before retiring in 1990, he drew up no fewer than 7,000 wills for coastal residents. For many years he did his own secretarial work. Kenneth was known to type seventy-two words per minute on his trusty manual typewriter. He made real estate work his other specialty and handled countless real estate transactions.[14] Kenneth always encouraged his clients to settle their differences out of court because it "would be easier on their nerves and pocketbook." He disliked the courtroom and frequently advised clients, "If you go to court, I'll hold your coat and hat."[15] A practical man, Kenneth advised his clients wishing to have their ashes dumped off the Yaquina Bay Bridge to specify they be scattered during "an outgoing tide so the ashes get

The Kenneth Litchfield family, August 1955. From left: Carol, Kenneth, Ruth, Frances, Ralph and Rich.
(Roger A. Hart)

Opposite: Kenneth Litchfield in his law office the year he retired, 1990.
(Bill Hall, News-Times)

out to sea."[16]

Kenneth also served as attorney for the City of Newport from 1940 into the 1960s. During World War II, Kenneth helped secure the lands needed for the construction of the airport at South Beach. In the 1970s, he moved his office to Highway 101 when he joined McPherson and Carstens. Kenneth retired in 1990.

Kenneth and Frances raised four children: Ruth, Carol, Ralph, and Rich. In the Litchfield tradition, all have moved away from Lincoln County. So far, Carol, wife of John Rehfuss, has been the first to carry on the second part of the Litchfield tradition: coming home again.

END NOTES
1. Paul and Henrietta R. Van de Velde, *South County and its Early Settlers, Vol. I, Charles L. Litchfield* (Newport: Lincoln County Historical Society), 4.
2. Bill Hall, "Litchfield Family Goes Back in County History," *News-Times*, 28 Feb. 1990.
3. Van de Velde, 4.
4. Fred Lockley, "In Earlier Days," *Oregon Journal*, 14 Feb. 1914.
5. Van de Velde, 4.
6. Ibid, 4-6.
7. Sharon SeaBrook, "PCH Foundation Receives Stock Donation from Ken and Frances Litchfield," *News-Times*, 12 Feb. 1997.
8. Bill Hall, "Ken Litchfield: Still Practicing Law Close to Home,"

News-Times, 28 Feb. 1990, Mature Lifestyles section.

9. "Kenneth Litchfield is Grand Marshal," *News-Times*, May 1982.

10. "Kenneth Litchfield to Enter Law Office in Toledo," *Lincoln County Leader*, 14 June 1928.

11. "Attorney Locates Here," *Newport Journal*, 19 June 1940.

12. Carmel Finley, "Longtime Newport Attorney Found Success Close to Home," *Oregonian*, 19 Sept. 1990.

13. "High Winds Hit Coast Areas," *Newport News*, 18 Oct. 1962.

14. Finley.

15. Hall, "Ken Litchfield: Still Practicing."

16. John Rehfuss, "Newport's King of Wills Remembered," *News-Times*, undated clipping, 1990.

MONTEREY HOTEL

AN ADVENTURER'S DREAM
TURNS TO GRIEF

In 1893, a stock market panic ushered in the worst economic depression of that century. Within a year's time, hundreds of the nation's banks had closed their doors, and unemployment skyrocketed to twenty percent.

It was in those dark days that John Fitzpatrick established the Monterey Hotel, the biggest, grandest resort hotel on the central Oregon Coast. Fitzpatrick had the lumber for the $75,000 hotel milled fifty miles away in Corvallis and shipped to its site north of Newport, next to Big Creek, in a small sheltered valley just a stone's throw from Agate Beach. One hundred forty acres of tree-covered grounds surrounded the Monterey.[1]

Apparently the Monterey was an immediate hit, particularly with vacationers from Salem who found "the immense beach, the free baths, the homelike comforts, and excellent service" rendered by the Fitzpatricks "made it a most desirable summer resort."[2] The Monterey also was described as "a charming retreat for invalids and health seekers."[3] Coastal vacationers of this era often believed

Opposite: The Monterey Hotel, ca. 1895. Built during the depression of the 1890s, the Monterey was the largest, grandest hotel on the central Oregon Coast.

breathing fresh ocean air and bathing in the surf had recuperative powers. Another attractive feature of the Monterey was its close proximity to the Yaquina Head Lighthouse, a popular tourist destination.

In 1893, both the lighthouse and the Monterey were chosen as destinations for 126 San Francisco merchants who toured the area to assess its economic prospects. After visiting the lighthouse, the group went to the newly completed hotel, where the Fitzpatrick family hosted a banquet.[4] After dinner the delegation proceeded to the next destination of its whirlwind tour. Less than a year later, the glory days of the Monterey were gone as well.

On the surface it may seem the Monterey was simply a victim of the depression of the 1890s. But the story of the Fitzpatricks and the events leading to the rise and tragic fall of the Monterey is far more intriguing than simple economics.

JOHN FITZPATRICK: ADVENTURER, FISHERMAN, SHREWD BUSINESSMAN

John Fitzpatrick was born in 1825 in Ireland. As a fairly young man, he took to the seas, ending up in Louisiana. He sailed again for two years, jumping ship in New York to take an inland job. Itching for adventure, Fitzpatrick enlisted in the Mexican-American War as an army seaman aboard the warship *Ohio* for a three-year hitch. When he was discharged in 1849 in San Francisco,

Yaquina Head Lighthouse, ca. 1900. The Monterey's close proximity to the lighthouse offered another incentive for prospective guests. (A.L. Thomas)

Fitzpatrick set out prospecting for gold on the American River. He met with success, accumulating a rather substantial fortune (in its day) of $10,000.

Apparently Fitzpatrick was an amiable man; in fact, his easy manner may have saved his life. One night he encountered a known killer, Joaquin Murrietta, who was being pursued by a posse. Fitzpatrick, who did not know of Murrietta or of the posse, offered him a meal and a blanket — probably his salvation, as Murrietta was known to have killed many indiscriminately along his way.

Seining on the Columbia River, early 1910s. John Fitzpatrick acquired seining grounds on the Columbia and was an accomplished fisherman.

According to a relative, Fitzpatrick once met a man who owned a fighting bulldog and an island called Deer Island. Fitzpatrick bought both from him "for some money and a gallon of liquor." Later he sold the dog but the island was undoubtedly a profitable investment.

His sights turned to Oregon when he met a man in a San Francisco bar who was preparing to head north to fish the Columbia River. Fitzpatrick followed him there and went on to prove himself an able Columbia River fisherman. He later became partners in a cannery near Megler, Washington, and acquired Fitzpatrick Sands seining grounds on the Columbia. Fitzpatrick has been credited with introducing the first power (steam) fishing boats on

The Monterey Hotel, ca. 1906. Because of isolation and tragedy, the Monterey's heyday was short-lived. A 1910 census shows no boarders or guests staying at the Monterey.

the Columbia.

While in Washington, Fitzpatrick married Mary DuCheney, a descendant of a Chinook Indian chief and twenty-five years younger than her groom. Together they had eight children. Twenty-six years after their marriage, sixty-nine-year-old Fitzpatrick died after contracting pneumonia on a trip on the Columbia. It has been said that Fitzpatrick cleared millions of dollars before his death in May 1894.[5]

Fitzpatrick's death came just a year or two after the Monterey Hotel was built. He had intended to continue fishing and have his wife and children run the hotel.[6] Fitzpatrick also planned to establish a cannery and a sawmill on the Siletz River. Despite Fitzpatrick's untimely death, his wife and children assumed operation of the hotel that had been named in honor of a Mexican War battle

Fitzpatrick participated in, the capturing of Monterey.[7]

TRAGEDY AT THE MONTEREY

Unfortunately, the economic depression of the 1890s held its grip on the nation for several years. Guests who could afford to pay for accommodations in a first-class modern hotel were few and far between. At this time, Agate Beach was several miles from town and isolated from Newport's two main areas of activity: Nye Beach and the Bayfront. In rainy weather, the dirt roads turned to mud. The beach was passable as a road but only at low tide.

Handicapped, the hotel limped along. A 1910 census entry shows Mary as the proprietor of the hotel; her daughter, Sarah, and one servant were its only residents. The fifty-room establishment had no registered guests or boarders at that time.[8]

Things may have looked as if they might improve in the early 1910s. Newport, like much of the nation, entered into an era of prosperity. Tourists flocked to the area, and new hotels and cottages popped up like weeds. Any possibility of a change in fortune for the Monterey, however, became unlikely after January 20, 1912. According to a newspaper account of the time, Sarah Fitzpatrick, twenty-five, was found dead in one of the rooms with a bullet wound through her heart. She was described as "an accomplished woman of fine attainments, well-educated, modest, and retiring and loved by all her acquaintances." The article added that "those who knew her best . . . feel that the bullet wound that caused her death was accidental."[9]

There are two unverifiable accounts of the circumstances of her death. A short article appearing in the local newspaper more than two decades after her death reported she was presumably murdered by parties unknown.[10] A second account claims her fiance from Portland called their marriage plans off and, grief-stricken, she went upstairs and shot herself.[11]

Prior to the tragedy, most of the Fitzpatrick children may have moved away from the area. But four months after Sarah's death, her sister, Rebecca, who owned a homestead upriver from Kernville, held her wedding at the Monterey.[12]

The hotel's chain of ownership is unclear, but just three months after Sarah's death, the Fitzpatrick family began negotiating a lease (or sale) with Joseph A. Hill of Hill Military Academy of Portland. Hill desired to established a branch of his academy at the troubled hotel.[13]

In 1900, Hill's father, Joseph W., "a Yale man," established the first private military school in the Northwest on thirty-eight lots in a residential area of Portland.[14] The curriculum included a mix of vocational training, military drills, and academic work.[15] By the time the academy branched out to the Monterey, Joseph W. had turned over the school's management to his son, Joseph A.

The details of the operation of Hill's Military

Academy are not known, but it appears the place doubled as an academy and as a hotel. In an attempt to put the Monterey's troubled past behind him, Hill changed its name to the Ocean Hill Hotel.[16] Perhaps for the first time, the hotel was kept open all year long.[17] In 1913, Hill constructed two additional buildings on the hotel grounds: a "clubhouse," complete with a reception hall with a circular fireplace, and a dining hall to be used by the academy summer camp.[18] (The fireplace was described as "the only one of that peculiar style north of Los Angeles.") Activity at the hotel picked up when the summer academy was in session. One account estimates about fifty cadets resided there in the summer months.[19] A few newspaper stories from the time reported that dances and banquets were held at the Ocean Hill, and Newport residents attended.[20] For a least

Ocean Hill Hotel, ca. 1913. Formerly the Monterey, the Ocean Hill Hotel doubled as an academy.

Above: The Ocean Hill Hotel, 1918. This trestle over Big Creek was built by construction workers from the Spruce Division, who set up tents on the hotel grounds, right.
(Above photo by C. Kinsey)

one year, Hill used his Studebaker-Garford car as a bus to transport patrons back and forth from the hotel.[21]

Even with a free ride to the hotel, the editor of the local paper may have been hesitant to venture to Ocean Hill. There was a certain dog there that apparently possessed a dislike for him. The editor's short report on his encounter with the unfriendly canine began, "Monday morning a dog from the Ocean Hill Hotel meandered into town and tried to bite a leg off the editor of this paper."[22]

During these active years at Ocean Hill, there was a small degree of military influence. The military presence increased when an army of construction workers from the Spruce Division began building a railroad trestle over Big Creek and the picturesque valley. Eventually this logging railroad line was completed as far north as Otter Rock. Construction workers set up tents on the hotel grounds. It seems likely the officers slept in the hotel. That part of the valley has since been filled in to accommodate Highway 101.[23]

It is not known exactly when or how, but the hotel passed into non-military management or ownership. The Rev. C.R. Ellsworth, who had been a minister and teacher on the Siletz Reservation,[24] and his wife, Susan, operated the hotel for at least a few years. It is not known exactly how long the Ellsworths ran the hotel, but by the time of his death in 1922, the reverend had left the Monterey and was running a hotel in Toledo and serving as a pastor.[25]

It appears that Mary Fitzpatrick remained at the

hotel despite the changes of ownership/management and the tragedies of its past.[26] Mary's son, John Fitzpatrick Jr., later returned to the area and lived with his mother at the Monterey until he died there in 1922 .[27] Mary finally left the area around 1927.

Mr. J.A. Robbins of Portland may have been the last person to attempt a successful operation at the Monterey. In 1926, he leased the hotel with intentions of developing an auto park and bringing in saddle horses from Pendleton for his guests to ride.[28] The final chapter of the Monterey story came in 1933. C. E. Chilton, who had purchased the Monterey in 1931, tore down the hotel to replace it with "several modern cottages"[29] which he later supplemented with a service station.[30]

The State of Oregon purchased this eighteen-acre parcel from the Lincoln County Development Company in 1969 and created day-use facilities at which visitors can picnic and access Agate Beach.[31]

While Fitzpatrick's dream of a first-class hotel called Monterey is indeed history, the establishment of the state park has enabled a part of the dream to live on: it remains a great place to relax, enjoy the beach, and escape from life's demands.

END NOTES
1. Jack Fogarty, "The Old Hostelries were Once Elegant," *Graphic Review,* 11 Aug. 1966.
2. "The Monterey," *Capital Journal,* 24 June 1894.
3. "The Monterey," *Capital Journal,* 30 June 1894.
4. "Visiting Valley Towns," *Oregonian*, 31 July 1893.
5. Charles Eastland to Bea Wilcox, 21 May 1974, Fitzpatrick

Biography File, Oregon Coast History Center Research Library, Newport.

6. Fogarty.

7. "The Death of Mr. John Fitzpatrick," *Lincoln County Leader*, 17 May 1894.

8. Jan McKee, comp., *1910 Lincoln County Census* (Eugene: Oregon Genealogical Society Inc.), 99.

9. "Died," *Lincoln County Leader*, 23 Jan. 1911.

10. "Another Ancient Landmark Passes," *Yaquina Bay News*, 12 Oct. 1933.

11. Ray Moe, "Newport's Former Monterey Hotel — Jilted Love and Other Tales," *News-Times*, 25 April 1990, Mature Lifestyles section.

12. "Married, Wood-Fitzpatrick," *Yaquina Bay News-Reporter*, 07 April 1910.

13. "Hill Military School May Open Branch at Newport," *Yaquina Bay News*, 18 April 1912.

14. Howard McKinley Corning, ed., *Dictionary of Oregon History* (Portland: Binford and Mort, 1956), 114.

15. W.H. Shelor, "A Pioneer in Secondary Education and His Work in the Pacific Northwest," *Pacific Monthly*, October 1900.

16. Untitled, *Yaquina Bay News*, 02 May 1912.

17. Untitled, *Yaquina Bay News*, 19 Sept. 1912.

18. "Ocean Hill Being Improved," *Yaquina Bay News*, 24 April 1913.

19. "Another Ancient Landmark."

20. Untitled, *Yaquina Bay News*, 24 July 1913.

21. Untitled, *Yaquina Bay News*, 25 June 1914.

22. Untitled, *Yaquina Bay News*, 25 Sept. 1913.

23. Lloyd Palmer, *Steam Towards the Sunset* (Newport: Lincoln County Historical Society, 1990), 38.

24. "Susan E. Ellsworth Called by Death," unknown newspaper and date, 1933.

25. "Rev. C. E. Ellsworth Passes," *Yaquina Bay News*, 11 Aug. 1922.

26. "Married, Aupperlee-Fitzpatrick," *Yaquina Bay News*, 02 May 1912.

27. "John P. Fitzpatrick Passes," *Yaquina Bay News*, 17 Aug. 1922.

28. "Monterey Leased," *Yaquina Bay News*, 24 June 1926.

29. "Another Ancient Landmark."

30. Moe.

31. Lawrence C. Merriam, et. al, *Oregon Parks System 1921-1989: An Administrative History* (Salem: Oregon State Parks, 1992), 149.

GUARDING THE COAST

YAQUINA BAY'S LIFE SAVERS

For more than one hundred years, the Yaquina Bay Coast Guard Station has been the landmark guardian of the central Oregon Coast. Its crews have helped countless ships in distress. They have patrolled hundreds of miles of beaches to ensure the safety of civilians. They have lost their lives while saving others.

The first U.S. Life Saving Service Station (predecessor to the Coast Guard) was constructed in 1896 on the beach about a mile south of Yaquina Bay's channel opening.[1] The station was a Marquette type, a standard government design of this period; thirteen such stations were built beginning in 1890, most of them in Michigan and Oregon.[2] The beach was chosen for two reasons: it was flat, enabling rescuers (surfmen) to launch their boats quickly; and most of the wrecks on Yaquina Bay occurred on the south side of the channel entrance.[3]

The men at the South Beach station spent hours each day walking up and down the beach, watching for

Above: Yaquina Life Saving Service pin from the 1910s.

Opposite: A thirty-six-foot Yaquina Bay Coast Guard lifeboat returning to station, 1946.

ships in distress. To monitor the patrols, the station commander required the men to punch a card at selected stations along the beach.[4] The boats were made of wood, but the men were made of iron: the men had to row enormous oars to propel their heavy wooden rescue boats. When the winds were favorable, however, they could hoist a sail to help them along.

One day in 1898, the South Beach crew was called upon to rescue a ship in distress. The sailing ship *Atalanta*, which was loaded with nearly 24,000 bags of wheat, hit a reef just south of Waldport's Alsea Bay.[5] Sixteen hours had elapsed before the surfmen were notified of the wreck. They hitched horses to the boats (which were kept on trailers in the boathouses) and headed south. The horses gave out before they reached Waldport. The crew did not reach the wreck until the next day, when the crisis was over.[6] This was long before the area had telegraphs, radios, and tele-

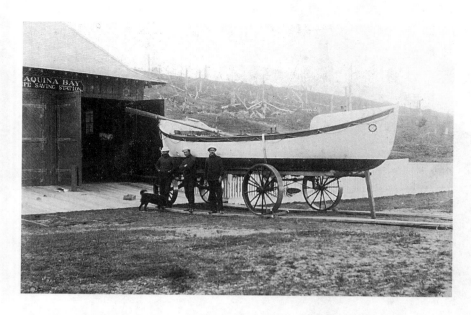

phones. There wasn't even a north-south road, with the exception of the beach and some trails.

In August 1906, the life savers moved closer to Newport's Bayfront when they took over the abandoned Yaquina Bay Lighthouse. The lighthouse had not been in service since 1874, when it was replaced by the Yaquina Head Lighthouse. The men must have favored the move. Not only were they closer to town, but beach patrols were discontinued: the tower atop the lighthouse offered a commanding view of the ocean. A newspaper of the day remarked, "The patrol duty is no longer necessary, which will be a great relief to the members of the crew as the exposure they were formerly subject to was very trying upon their health."[7]

Not only was the old lighthouse equipped with an observation tower, it also contained living quarters for

Above: In the 1890s, the Life Saving Service kept its boats on trailers that could be hitched to horses for land transport. This is the first station, built at South Beach.

Opposite, top: The first Yaquina Bay Life Saving Service crew, 1896. From left, front row: Frank Ayerde, Capt. O.S. Wicklund, and Albert Beyer. Back row: Victor Peterson, Jack Fogarty, O.F. Jacobson, Walter Whitten, and William Bullus. Opposite, bottom: An early U.S.L.S.S. patch.

unmarried crewmen.[10] The married men and their families took up residence at the Ocean House Hotel on the Bayfront (site of the present Coast Guard Station). A boathouse eventually was constructed on the Bayfront, in about the same location as the present-day boathouse.[11] For a few years after the move, a couple of backup boats were maintained at the old South Beach station.[12]

With the move came the end of a popular trail among locals known as "Lover's Lane."[8] Seclusion could be found on the trail that wound its way through the dense trees and brush between the Ocean House Hotel to the old lighthouse. The trail was widened and covered with wood planks to allow wagon traffic to reach the new station.[9]

In 1914, the Life Saving Service acquired its first powerboat, the *Undaunted.* Built of mahogany and oak, this thirty-six-foot, self-righting craft was equipped with a forty-horsepower gasoline engine and an electric search light. It was "superior to any other boat on the coast."[13] At that time, the Yaquina Bay Station had the only power rescue boat between the Columbia River and Bandon. Even with a motor rescue boat, the Life Saving Service (renamed the Coast Guard in 1915) was still supplementing its rescue fleet with oar-powered boats into the late 1920s.

In 1932, the Coast Guard built a new station.[14] It was located at the west end of Bay Boulevard, on the bay side, near the base of the hill where the current station sits. This land appears to have been purchased by the City of Newport in the 1910s and given to the Coast Guard

Opposite: The first Life Saving Service Station at South Beach, ca. 1900.

Below: The Life Saving Service took over the abandoned Yaquina Bay Lighthouse in 1906.

for the purpose of establishing a station. The station was constructed and fully equipped, including quarters for the entire crew, a kitchen, a dining room, and a boat house, for $24,000.[15]

Just three years after it moved into the new Bayfront station, the Yaquina Bay Coast Guard experienced perhaps its worst tragedy. A crew in a thirty-six-foot motor lifeboat responded to a distress signal from a tug towing a dredge in the Yaquina Bay channel. While the Coast Guard men were struggling to pull a civilian from the water into their lifeboat, it was hit by a wave and capsized. Without warning, seven men, two of them civilians, found themselves in the frigid waters. Only two survived: Eldred Halsey and John Hart, both Coast Guard men.[16] (Halsey later wrote an account of these events which was published by the Lincoln County Historical Society titled, *Tragedy on Yaquina Bar*.) The Coast Guard quickly regrouped. Within a week, five additional men were transferred to the Yaquina Bay Station, and a new lifeboat was brought from Astoria.[17]

The Yaquina Bay Coast Guard built this station in 1932 on the west end of Bay Boulevard, near the base of the hill where the current station sits.

In 1936, a lookout tower was constructed next to the old Yaquina Bay Lighthouse station.[18] Plans also were made to establish an auxiliary station at Depoe Bay.[19] In 1941, a substantial addition was made to the Newport station, making it one of the biggest and best-equipped Coast Guard stations on the Oregon Coast.[20]

Perhaps it was because this station was state-of-the-art that it became a hub of activity during World War II. When the United States entered the war, a special division of the Coast Guard was created called the Beach Patrol. Its function was to patrol the nation's beaches in search of any signs of enemy invasion. In later years, these patrols of armed men were sometimes on horseback or accompanied by German shepherd dogs.[21] When Richard Van Hine was made commander of the Yaquina Bay Station in 1943, he found himself supervising 582 men, most of them members of the Beach Patrol.[22] His jurisdiction stretched as far north as Pacific City and as far south as the Umpqua River.[23]

During World War II, the Coast Guard's Beach Patrol kept watch for signs of possible enemy invasion. This picture was taken in 1942-43 at Tahkenitch Lake.

One of the Coast Guard's Beach Patrol stations was at the Spouting Horn at Depoe Bay. This picture was taken in 1943.

Some of the Lincoln County Beach Patrol stations were located at Nelscott, Depoe Bay (at the Spouting Horn Restaurant), Cape Foulweather (at the Lookout), Yaquina Head Lighthouse, and Waldport (at the Waldport Auto Court). As the war progressed, the chances of an invasion decreased; in February 1944, the government scaled down Beach Patrols by 50 percent.[24]

Just a month before, the Yaquina Bay Station had been destroyed by fire. Of unknown origin, the fire spread through the station rapidly on and under the first floor. The Newport Fire Department, Coast Guard personnel, and the Toledo Fire Department combined efforts to control the blaze. The station was a total loss. The heat had been so intense that buildings across the street were scorched and their windows broken. Only one crew member was slightly injured.

Although the station burned to the ground, all of the motorized equipment was saved.[25] The crew of the Yaquina Bay Station took up residence temporarily at the Abbey Hotel while arrangements for a new facility were made.[26] The Coast Guard leased land from the Newport American Legion on Harbor Drive between what was then Third and Fourth streets (now Eleventh and Tenth streets).

This was in the area where Newport's hospital is now located. Six barrack-type buildings were trucked in from another military installation to serve as the new station.

Despite an inadequate facility, the work of the Coast Guard continued. One of the more dramatic rescues of this time period took place at Vanport, a company-built town of nearly ten thousand houses in Multnomah County built to serve World War II workers. The town flooded on May 30, 1948, when a dike gave way. The first boat on the scene was a Yaquina Bay surf boat that happened to be in the area. Under the command of Chief Boatswain's Mate John A. Woodworth, the crewmen rescued seventeen people in one hour. They remained on the scene for several days, rescuing "a miscellany of dogs, cats, chickens, as well as three horses."[27]

About this time, the Yaquina Bay Coast Guard made plans to shift its operations to a new facility and return the property to the American Legion.[28] In December 1949, construction of a new facility on Naterlin Drive was completed. Sen. Guy Gordon was credited with obtaining a construction appropriation.[29] The original main building of this complex remains in use to this day. The Newport American Legion received its land back with the vacated buildings in lieu of

In January 1944, the Yaquina Bay Station was destroyed by fire. The Coast Guard was housed at the Abbey Hotel, then in barracks before a new station was completed in 1949.

The Coast Guard station on Naterlin Drive, 1949. The main building is still in use today.

restoration of the property and rent. The Legion planned to use one of the buildings as a youth center.[30] On the site of the burned station, a new Coast Guard dock was constructed.

Over the years, many changes have come to this station, but the exterior of the main building remains largely unchanged. Originally a shop facility was built nearby, but this was torn down and replaced with a larger building that serves as a mess hall and living quarters. The Coast Guard's boathouse on the bay was taken out in 1979 by a Peruvian freighter, the *Inca-Huayayna-Capac*. It had lost control of its wheel and rammed into the boathouse, destroying it.[31]

The station received national attention in 1977 when Master Chief Boatswain's Mate Tom McAdams announced his retirement. McAdams, who had been in the Coast Guard for twenty-seven years, achieved the highest enlisted rank. McAdams was a world-renowned sea rescue expert and a surf boat test pilot who helped design the Coast Guard's forty-four-foot rescue boat. He had been in charge of the Yaquina Bay station for three years, the maximum duration the Coast Guard allows at a station. Upon his retirement, he was awarded the Legion of Merit, one of the Coast Guard's highest awards.[32] CBS news correspondent Charles Kuralt came to Newport and spent a couple of days interviewing and filming McAdams for a story on his "On the Road" program.[33]

The members of the Yaquina Bay Station received honors in 1983 for their heroic efforts in rescuing all nineteen of the crewmen of the freighter *Blue Magpie*. It ran aground into the Yaquina Bay jetty in heavy seas. Personnel worked for hours in extremely turbulent waters; the rescue was carried out without a hitch. During the following days they worked to clean the oil that spilled in the bay as the freighter broke up.[34]

For the *Blue Magpie* and other search and rescue efforts, the helicopter proved itself invaluable. Helicopters had not been a full-time part of the Yaquina Bay Station life-saving arsenal until 1994. After a great deal of lobbying effort by the Newport Fishermen's Wives and other concerned individuals, a helicopter landing pad was constructed at the Newport airport. A helicopter is now on call from the airport twenty-four hours a day. [35]

Over the years, the Coast Guard's responsibilities have grown to include law enforcement. Its jurisdictions include drug smuggling, violations of fisheries laws and the endangered species act, illegal immigration, violations of safety and environmental protection laws, and other federal criminal activity. Its original function, however, remains utmost in importance: to be a vigilant guardian of the central Oregon Coast.

The fifty-two-foot motor lifeboat Victory, *the oldest boat of this type still in service, 1957.*

END NOTES
1. Pernot S. Duff, "Yaquina Bay Lifesaving Station Tales," *Oregonian*, 18 March 1951.
2. Ralph Shanks and Wick York, *The United States Lifesaving Service* (Petaluma: Costano Books, 1996), 246.
3. Ibid, 32.
4. "In New Quarters," *Yaquina Bay News*, 16 Aug. 1906.
5. "The Sailor Report," *Lincoln County Leader,* 25 Nov. 1898.
6. Duff.
7. "In New Quarters."
8. Ibid.
9. Ibid.
10. "Life Saving Station Transferred," *Yaquina Bay News*, 02 Aug. 1906.
11. "Removal of U.S.L.S. Boat House Underway," *Yaquina Bay News-Reporter,* 23 Sept. 1909.
12. "Coast Guard Boat House Burned," *Yaquina Bay News*, 14 Aug. 1930.
13. "New Life Saving Power Boat Arrives," *Yaquina Bay News*, 12 March 1914.
14. "Coast Guard Station Inspected," *Yaquina Bay News*, 09 June 1932.
15. "New Station Officially Dedicated," *Newport Journal*, 06 April 1932.
16. Eldred Halsey, *Tragedy on Yaquina Bar* (Newport: Lincoln County Historical Society, 1988).
17. "New Coast Guard Boat Sent Here," *Yaquina Bay News*, 07 March 1935.
18. "New Look-out Station In Service," *Newport Journal*, 18 March 1936.
19. "Will Inspect Depoe Bay," *Newport Journal*, 01 Feb. 1939.
20. "Yaquina Bay Coast Guard Station Burns to the Ground," *Yaquina Bay News*, 06 Jan. 1944.
21. Dennis L. Noble, *The U.S. Coast Guard in World War II, The*

Beach Patrol and Corsair Fleet (Washington, DC: Coast Guard Historian's Office, 1992), 12.

22. David Lehman, "Man of the Sea," *Newport News-Times,* undated, 1990.

23. Leslie Glode, "Dick Van Hine Enjoys Life," *Newport News-Times,* 12 Feb. 1986.

24. Noble, 20.

25. "Yaquina Bay Coast Guard Station Burns . . ."

26. "New Building for Coast Guard Soon," *Newport News,* 30 Dec. 1948.

27. "Local Boat Praised For Flood Work," *Newport News,* 10 June 1948.

28. "Legion Gets Coast Guard Station Back," *Newport News,* 22 Dec. 1949.

29. "Portion of Funds For Coast Guard May Be Granted," *Newport News,* 10 June 1948.

30. "Youth Recreation Center Initial Aim in Converting Old Buildings," *Newport News,* 08 Dec. 1948.

31. "Freighter Struck Boat House In '79," *Newport News-Times,* 21 Nov. 1983.

32. "Yaquina Bay's Guard Chief to 'Hang Up' Rescue Helmet," *Capital Journal,* 08 Nov. 1976.

33. "New Honors Await Chief Tom McAdams," *Newport News-Times,* June 1977.

34. Peter Sleeth, "Freighter Runs Aground Off North Jetty, Crew Rescued; Cleanup Operation Begins," *Newport News-Times,* 21 Nov. 1983.

35. Leslie O'Donnell, "Local Efforts Bring Coast Guard Helicopter to Newport Airport," *Newport News-Times,* 25 July 1990.

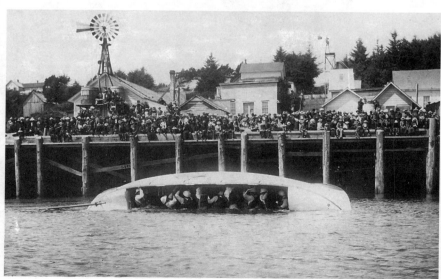

Life Saving Service capsize drill at the Bayfront, 1898.

OREGON BEACHES
THE SAND OF OS

An "outsider" often means a recent arrival who must become wise to local ways before he will be accepted. In the case of Oregon Gov. Oswald West (1873-1960), a foreign-born political outsider, it meant someone with a newcomer's perspective who was unwilling to accept the corrupt ways of doing business in Oregon in the early 1910s.

West possessed the drive and political acumen necessary to work his way into a position to affect change. The story of how West gained the governorship and what he accomplished while in office is nothing short of remarkable. Perhaps Governor "Os" West's greatest legacy is Oregon's publicly owned beaches. West maneuvered Oregon legislators into designating Oregon's beaches free and open to the public without them even knowing it.

West was born in Canada. He traveled to Oregon at age four with his parents and six siblings. They took up residence in Portland's Cosmopolitan Hotel. When the hotel went up in flames, the West family lost almost everything and was practically destitute. The Wests then moved to Roseburg briefly and in 1877 relocated to Salem, where

Opposite: Governor Oswald "Os" West at the Abbey Hotel in Newport, 1912. Seven months after his visit to Nye Beach, West orchestrated the passing of a bill declaring Oregon's seashore a public highway. (F.F. Sasman)

Oswald's father bought and sold livestock. In 1883, they moved back to Portland. Oswald, then a lad of ten, spent his days in school and evenings driving livestock through what is now downtown Portland. The family moved yet again, this time back to Salem, continuing in the livestock trade. By then West was old enough to drive a butcher's delivery wagon. At age sixteen his schooling was considered complete and he became a "discriminating student in the school of experience."[1]

He found employment as a messenger in the Ladd and Bush Bank. West worked his way up to the position of "paying teller."[2] While working at the bank, he witnessed legislators depositing bribe money. The bribes were compensation for the legislators' involvement in schemes that resulted in the theft of publicly owned land and timber.[3]

West then left the bank for Alaska, possibly out of disgust or a yearning for adventure. There he spent six months with pick and shovel in hand on a fruitless search for gold. West returned to the Salem bank only to move on to First National Bank of Astoria. In 1903, Oregon Governor Chamberlin appointed him to the Land Commission, where he investigated many a shady land deal. West later was appointed to the Railroad Commission. He earned a reputation as being a man of action who was "prompt and persistent in efforts to establish a better order of things."[4]

Perhaps because of the shady land deals that seemed prevalent wherever he went, West took a job as state land agent. He did not aspire for the governorship until he happened upon a political rally in Portland. When West saw that many of the rally participants were the same men whose bribe deposits he had processed at the Salem bank, he threw his hat in the race.[5]

He began his campaign with practically no money, well-connected friends, or political machine to back him. West wrote of his campaign, "I was not a just a poor speaker, I was a lousy one." Because of his inexperience he set his sights on Central Oregon, "where the voters were few and charitable." West ran on a prohibitionist platform, promising a clean government beyond the influence of corporations. He billed himself as "the man who delivers the goods." After traveling the state and running up campaign expenses totaling $3,804.60, West was elected governor by a 6,700-vote margin.[6]

In June 1912, a year and a half after he was elected, West traveled to Newport for the opening ceremonies of the recently completed Nicolai Hotel. When word got out the governor would attend the hotel's opening, the entire town was decorated along with every room in the Nicolai. (Unfortunately, rain "spoiled the effect" of the outdoor adornments.[7]) West took the train first to Yaquina City, where a party of celebrants awaited his arrival. Flag-waving schoolchildren sang the national anthem and Siletz Indians in full regalia danced for the governor before he boarded the ferry for Newport.[8]

Seventy-five people (about ten percent of

Newport's population) gathered for a banquet and ball at the Nicolai. Featured speakers were Newport Mayor George Wilcox, Southern Pacific Railroad representative John M. Scott, and Governor West. The governor did not speak about his plans (if he had any then) for Oregon's beaches. Instead, he spoke on one of the controversial issues of the day: women's right to vote.[9] Governor West had been a strong supporter of women's right to vote ever since he was ten years old, when he happened upon a small crowd gathered on a Salem street to listen to noted suffragette Abigail Scott Duniway. She looked down upon the ragged, barefoot boy and asked him, "Don't you consider your mother as good, if not better, than an ordinary saloon bum?" West replied softly, "Sure I do." When Oregon voters approved women's suffrage five months after Governor West's Newport stay, he assigned the elderly Duniway the honor of preparing the document for his signature.[10]

Nicolai Hotel on Nye Beach, ca. 1912.

After the speeches, the guests retired to the Nicolai ballroom, "where those who so desired trip't the fantastic toe to the delightful strains of Branch's Orchestra."[11]

Newspaper accounts portray West's Newport

In the photograph, handwritten text reads: "GOV. WEST and S. L. S. NEWPORT ORE."

visit as enjoyable for all parties concerned. It is not known if his trip to Nye Beach inspired him to take action to preserve and protect Oregon's beaches, but it was seven months after West returned from Newport that he wrote a concise, sixty-word bill declaring the Oregon seashore a public highway. He proposed this bill knowing a real road would eventually replace the beach. West also knew that once the Highway Commission (which he created even though the state had no highways) had control of the beaches, it would never let the seashore back into the private sector.

From his experience with land fraud investigations, West knew Oregon's beaches were vulnerable. West want-

Governor West with the U.S. Life Saving Service in Newport during his 1912 visit. From left: Crosby Mathews, (possibly) Beryl King, D. Dunn, Joe Briggs, Governor West, Anton Gustafson, Rich Chattenton, August Blatner, and Billy Kellhaus. (F.F. Sasman)

113

Oregon's beaches had served as public highways since the first horse-drawn wagon was introduced on the coast. This one is pulling sightseers along Nye Beach near Jump-Off Joe, ca. 1905.

ed the state to take control of the beaches, even though he knew the Republican-dominated legislature would not support this idea. West prevailed, using a combination of political stealth and deception. The bill was perceived by the lawmakers as routine and it became law with practically no debate.[12] After all, the beach had served as a tide-dependent highway ever since the first horse-drawn wagon was introduced on the coast.

West's legislation remained unchanged until 1947, when the Oregon Legislature quietly changed the designation of Oregon beaches from "highway" to "recreation area." Perhaps in this same piece of 1947 legislation, the Highway Commission was given the authority to grant permits for removing sand and rock from the beaches. When permission was given to remove smelt sands along the Yachats River for a construction project, the aging ex-governor West went to bat for Oregon's beaches once again. At a highway commission meeting, West proclaimed, "As long as God gives me strength, nobody is going to remove a shovelful of sand, a shovelful of rocks from those beaches."[13] This attempt to remove the smelt sands was stopped shortly thereafter.

No major threats to access or public ownership of

Oregon's beaches occurred in West's lifetime. He died quietly in his sleep in 1960. Two years before his death, he was honored when Short Sand Beach Park, a 2,474-acre state facility in Clatsop and Tillamook counties, was renamed Oswald West State Park.[14]

Nye Beach, 1920s. The thousands of visitors who flock to Oregon's publicly owned beaches can thank Governor West. (A.L. Thomas)

Oregon residents and the thousands of visitors who flock to its beaches are indeed fortunate that Gov. Oswald West lived up to his campaign pledge to be "the man who delivers the goods."

END NOTES
1. Joseph Gaston, *The Centennial History of Oregon 1811-1912*, vol. 2 (Chicago: The S.J. Clarke Company Publishing Company), 262.
2. Ibid, 263.
3. Brent Walth, *Fire At Eden Gate: Tom McCall and the Oregon Story* (Portland: Oregon Historical Society Press, 1994), 184.
4. Gaston, 262.
5. Walth, 184.
6. Oswald West, "Reminiscences and Anecdotes: Political History," *Oregon Historical Quarterly*, vol. 50, No. 4, Dec. 1949, 243-245.
7. "Gov. West at the Beach," *Yaquina Bay News*, 20 June 1912.
8. Ibid.
9. "The Nicolai Formally Opened," *Yaquina Bay News*, 27 June 1912.
10. West, 249.
11. "The Nicolai."
12. Harold Hughes, "Crafty Os West Hoodwinked Legislature To Get Sandy Beaches For State," *Sunday Oregonian*, 14 May 1967.
13. "Spoilage of Oregon Beaches Opposed at Hearing: Local Groups Join Protest," *Newport News*, 01 Jan. 1948.
14. Lawrence C. Merriam, et. al, *Oregon Parks System 1921-1989: An Administrative History* (Salem: Oregon State Parks, 1992), 209.

PUBLICITY STUNTS & PUBLIC WORKS

THE PATHFINDERS

A new age dawned in the early 1900s: the age of the automobile. Much of the country shifted suddenly into high gear. The freedom afforded by the automobile changed our society: towns were reshaped, and auto-related businesses sprang up.

Lincoln County, on the other hand, had been bypassed — at least this was the opinion of the Newport Commercial Club, forerunner of today's Chamber of Commerce. At the time, few could argue with this assertion. What is now Highway 20 could be traveled only a few months of the year. There were no roads to the south or north of Newport, except for the beach. Travel was dependent on the tides, making it a dangerous proposition. Inexperienced motorists often were tempted to drive on the smooth, wet sand near the water, but the incoming ocean waves frequently left soft places in the sand that would stop a car in its tracks. More than a few motorists wound up with their cars embedded in the sand, then lost during

Opposite: The "Pathfinders," as they were known, became the first to drive a car from Newport to Siletz Bay and back in 1912. The trek was sponsored by the Commercial Club as a publicity stunt to draw attention to Lincoln County's poor road system.

117

The Pathfinders began their historic trek at the Abbey Hotel in Newport at 7:35 a.m. Saturday, July 20, 1912. The trip to Siletz Bay and back took twenty-three hours.

an incoming tide.[1]

To generate awareness of the sad state of Lincoln County's roads, the Commercial Club organized a unique publicity stunt that has become the stuff of local legend. A Studebaker dealer in Portland, EMF Auto Company, was persuaded to supply a Flanders 20 automobile for "the first automobile trip from Newport to Siletz Bay." William "Will" Burton organized the trip for the Commercial Club; other members of the "Pathfinders" party were T.F. Kershaw, editor of the short-lived *Newport Signal* newspaper; Fred F. Sasman, professional photographer who documented the trip; and J.D. Grant, an experienced cross-country driver. The car was equipped for the off-road adventure with a windlass on the front bumper and was loaded down with picks, shovels, axes, saws, gas, oil, food, blackberry brandy, and beer.

At 7:35 a.m. on Saturday, July 20, 1912, the Pathfinders left Newport's Abbey Hotel to venture where no automobile had been before — the Siletz Bay — and return home. An account of the trip, which took nearly twenty-three hours, appeared in two articles in the

Portland newspaper, the *Oregon Journal*. The July 27 edition included a full-page article in the automotive section complete with seven of Sasman's photographs.[2] The local paper, the *Yaquina Bay News*, did not give the trip a mention — perhaps because T.F. Kershaw's paper had been a competing publication. Despite the efforts of the Pathfinders to jump-start interest in improving roads, it would be another fifteen years before the route they pioneered could be traversed by auto.

Reportedly, some of the people the Pathfinders encountered on their trip had never seen a car.[3] In this era, the automobile was a novelty — especially in rural areas such as Lincoln County. In Newport, the arrival of the first car each year was a newsworthy event. The first car of 1911 rolled into Newport in April. An account of the event appeared in the local paper. The "big" thirty-horsepower touring car owned by Pacific Telephone and Telegraph Company made the journey from Eugene "without an accident, but attended by some difficulty." The trip required an overnight stop in Wren. After getting bogged down in mud up to the car's axles several times, "both men and auto,

The Pathfinders used every trick imaginable to hoist, pull, drag, and leverage their car over the most treacherous parts of the trip.

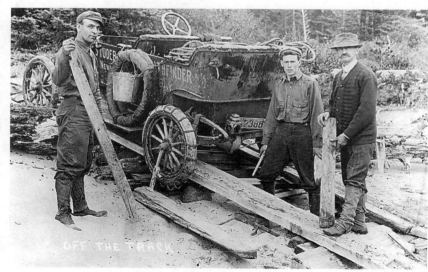

liberally coated with mud . . . arrived in Newport."[4] In the 1960s, Jack Fogarty recalled that one of the first cars to make the trip between Toledo and Newport in 1912 made the journey on the foredeck of his steamer, the *Truant*.[5]

With the advent of automobile assembly-line production, prices dropped and ownership skyrocketed. In 1912, only one in sixty-six Oregonians owned an automobile.[6] By 1919, one in every nine Oregonians owned one.[7] In Lincoln County, the rate of automobile ownership probably was much lower: the lack of roads also made auto ownership impractical. When at last almost anyone could afford an automobile, people began clamoring for better roads. In 1919, the Oregon Legislature passed a one-cent-per-gallon tax on gasoline, the first such tax in the nation. Proceeds from this innovative tax were dedicated toward road construction.[8]

The Pathfinders' Flanders 20 automobile was specially equipped with a windlass (hoist) and chains to help conquer the mud.

That same legislative session, Lincoln and Polk Counties Rep. Ben F. Jones introduced Oregon House Bill 147, which would put before the voters a measure authorizing construction of a road along the coast from Astoria to the California line called

the Roosevelt Military Highway.[9] Four months later, Oregon voters approved funding for the coast highway by a two-to-one margin.[10] The name "Military" was applied to this road, now known as Highway 101, to help persuade the federal government to fund fifty percent because this route was essential for defense purposes.[11]

When the Pathfinders finally reached Siletz, they celebrated with a banquet complete with "Salem" beer and blackberry brandy.

Survey work for the highway route first blazed by the Pathfinders in 1912 did not get under way until July 1922.[12] In summer 1923, work was in full swing. Camps of workers were scattered along the construction route for ten miles north of Newport. The local paper remarked, "Practically every man and boy over fourteen years of age is employed on this road in some capacity, while most of the women are milking the cows and doing the chores."[13]

The last section to be built was the most difficult: the stretch from Rocky Creek to the Siletz River. Rocky Creek was also the most challenging section for the Pathfinders of 1912: "The drop down to Rocky Creek was done with all brakes set . . . the slightest miscalculation would have precipitated the car into the ocean 300 or 400 feet below." It took the Pathfinders more than two hours to

The Siletz Bay, where the Pathfinders turned around, was bridged as part of the Roosevelt Military Highway project in 1927. This span at Kernville was replaced in 1974. (Stan Allyn)

climb to the top of Cape Foulweather (then called Bald Knob). The drive down the other side took eleven minutes.[14] For the road builders of 1925, this section also proved dangerous: a slide buried their steam shovel with eight feet of dirt and rocks.[15] The rickety wood bridge the Pathfinders used to cross Rocky Creek was replaced with the Ben Jones Bridge in June 1927.[16] The Siletz Bay, where the Pathfinders turned around, was also bridged as a part of this project.[17]

The Ben Jones, Siletz Bay, and Depoe Bay bridges were designed by Conde B. McCullough, designer of the Yaquina Bay Bridge. Construction to points south of Newport did not even begin until 1928 and were not completed until about 1930.

Thanks to the efforts of the Pathfinders and others who joined the "Good Roads" cause, automobilists have enjoyed easy access between Newport and Portland for more than seven decades. But as time passes, there is more and more debate on the ability of Highway 101 to meet current and future traffic demands. Perhaps the next generation of pathfinders will find ways to improve road safety or develop alternative transportation.

END NOTES

1. "Autoist Should be Careful," *Yaquina Bay News*, 22 July 1922.

2. J.E. Stembridge, ed., *Pathfinder: The First Automobile Trip From Newport to Siletz Bay, Oregon, July 1912* (Newport: Lincoln County Historical Society, 1975).

3. Stembridge, 16.

4. "First Auto of the Season," *Newport Signal*, 27 April 1911.

5. Jack Fogarty, untitled, *Newport Graphic Review*, 18 Aug. 1966.

6. Ben W. Olcott, comp., *State of Oregon List of Motor Vehicle Registrations and Transfers and Chauffeur Registrations and Convictions* (Salem: State Printer, 1912).

7. Ben W. Olcott, comp., *State of Oregon List of Motor Vehicle Registrations and Transfers and Chauffeur Registrations and Convictions* (Salem: State Printer, 1919).

8. Dwight A. Smith, James B. Norman, Pieter T. Dykman, *Historic Highway Bridges of Oregon* (Portland: Oregon Historical Society Press, 1989), 33.

Depoe Bay Bridge, ca. 1927. Along with the Siletz, Ben Jones, and Yaquina Bay bridges, this bridge was designed by Conde B. McCullough.

9. "Roosevelt Highway Proposed By B.F. Jones," *Yaquina Bay News*, 23 Jan. 1919.

10. "Roosevelt Highway Carries," *Yaquina Bay News*, 5 June 1919.

11. "Roosevelt Military Highway Bill Passed," *Yaquina Bay News*, 27 Feb. 1919.

12. "Roosevelt Survey Ordered From Newport North," *Yaquina Bay News*, 27 July 1922.

13. "Roosevelt Highway is Making Good Progress," *Yaquina Bay News*, 26 July 1923.

14. Stembridge, 21.

15. "Another Slide on Roosevelt Highway," *Yaquina Bay News*, 13 Aug. 1925.

16. "B.F. Jones Memorial Bridge Will be Dedicated," *Yaquina Bay News*, 11 Aug. 1927.

17. "Siletz Bridge Ready Soon," *Yaquina Bay News*, 18 Nov. 1926.

Adventures in Motoring

The Highway 20 Story

You may curse Highway 20 as you drive its narrow, winding curves in the rain with a tailgater behind you or a motor home in front that refuses to pull over; but it's the quickest way to the Willamette Valley from Newport. Once Highway 20 was just a trail, then a toll road; by 1943, however, it had become an interstate highway stretching from the Atlantic Ocean to the Pacific. The Highway 20 story involves moneymaking, government intervention, oysters, a great deal of mud, daring drivers, some "shoeless" legislation, and a new tax.

For hundreds of years before anyone dreamed of driving a car to the coast, Highway 20 was a trail along the banks of the Yaquina River traveled by local Indians. After the discovery of rich Yaquina Bay oyster beds in 1864, a group of settlers proposed a toll road from Corvallis to Elk City, the head of navigation on the Yaquina River. Early organizers called this forty-five-mile route the Yaquina Bay Military Wagon Road. In 1866, just a few months after

Opposite: A sign for Highway 20 reads, "See All of Oregon — You'll Like It! Turn Right at Newport." Above: A pin from the 1960s pleading for spiritual support was popular among locals who braved the twists and turns of Highway 20.

125

A little mud on the Toledo-Siletz mail stage

The Toledo-Siletz Mail Stage stuck in the mud near Toledo, ca. 1915. Between the mud and prolific coastal vegetation, keeping the route open was no easy task. (Cooper)

Yaquina Bay officially opened for white settlement, toll road construction was completed.[1] At Little Elk, a fifty-cent toll fee was levied for each team of animals and a twenty-five-cent fee for each person on horseback.[2] Toll road operators eventually received a government land grant of six miles on either side of the road to sell and use the proceeds to maintain the road. When operators could not find a buyer, the land was transferred to T. Egenton Hogg, who used the lands and its proceeds for a railroad line from Corvallis to Yaquina City (six miles east of Newport).[3]

Between the mud and rapidly growing coastal vegetation, keeping this route open was no easy task. By the 1880s, this responsibility had been assumed by Benton County. It was the goal of the county to maintain the road in "such a condition that a good team may travel from end to end of it in ten hours." The County Commissioners published a list of citizens who were required to work on the road. If someone was unable to work, he could "donate" money or supplies such as flour, bacon, beans, or coffee to help sustain the work parties.[4]

It is not known when the first automobile ventured from the Willamette Valley to Newport. One early-day motorist willing to take on the coastal road was Colonel Hofer of Salem. In July 1913, Hofer and his family motored from their Salem home through Kings Valley to Blodgett, Little Elk, Eddyville, Toledo, and on to Newport's Agate Beach. They left Salem at 8:20 a.m. and arrived at Agate Beach at 6:20 that evening, a ten-hour journey. Hofer had to stop and chain up on the muddy mountains between Blodgett and Eddyville and again over Pioneer Mountain. Hofer's automobile was the first to make it from the Willamette Valley that year -- and this was in the middle of summer. The return trip, in a steady rain, took nearly eleven hours of driving time. Hofer noted that while it was an exciting trip, he and his family suffered no hardships.[5]

At the time of Hofer's trip, the rail line was the easiest way to travel to the coast or transport goods. But given a choice, travelers of the late 1910s would rather not be confined to a train schedule. The auto was the rage; nearly everyone wanted and could afford the freedom of movement an automobile delivered. In 1913, assembly-line production was introduced by Henry Ford, driving the price of

The nation's first state gas tax, levied by the Oregon Legislature in 1919, helped make Highway 20 an all-weather road. Shown here is highway construction near Hill Street in Toledo, ca. 1920. This section was bypassed in 1966.

a new Model T from $850 down to $440.[6] Muddy roads that could be traveled only a few months out of the year kept enthusiasm for the auto in check in this region, however.

A new route for automobile traffic on Highway 20 was chosen in 1917.[7] Two years later, a bond measure passed to make this an all-weather road. An agreement was forged between Lincoln and Benton counties and the State Highway Commission. The counties assumed responsibility for doing the grading work and the state agreed to rock the road.[8] Beginning in 1919, funding for this and other road construction was generated from a new tax approved by the Oregon Legislature on each gallon of gasoline sold. Oregon was the first state in the Union to levy a gas tax. In the two decades that followed, mileage of all-weather roads in Oregon increased by 250 percent.[9]

(Before construction began on Highway 20, the citizens of Elk City signed a petition to relocate the Newport-Corvallis Highway along the Yaquina River through Elk City.[10] They were unsuccessful.)

Highway 20 was constructed with steam-powered and horse-powered equipment along with a great deal of manpower. By 1921, road conditions on Highway 20 were good enough that rumors began circulating about the possibility of bus service between Corvallis and Newport. On May 21, 1921, at 5 p.m., the first "auto stage" rolled into Newport. The fifteen-passenger CMC car began the inaugural trip in Albany at 9 a.m. It was projected that when the driver became familiar with the road, travel time between Albany and Newport would typically be between three and four hours.[11] The following month, a competing bus line started running a seven-passenger Studebaker on the Albany-Corvallis-Newport route. Bus stops in Newport were established at the post office and the Gilmore Hotel.[12]

Bus service on Highway 20 from Corvallis to Newport began in the 1920s, though it wasn't without its mishaps -- as this 1920s picture demonstrates.

After two more years of road improvements, year-round bus service began. By 1924, three buses a day were running between the valley and the coast. That same year, 4,500 cars arrived from Corvallis for a Fourth of July celebration. The previous year, only 400 cars made the trip.[13]

As the popularity of traveling to the coast by automobile increased, traffic on the railroad decreased. In 1928, the Southern Pacific Railroad Co. announced its line between Albany and Corvallis was losing money; to cut costs, it would no longer run separate passenger and freight trains. This slowed train service for shippers and passengers alike. Consequently, passenger traffic decreased, and freight tonnage diminished. Trucks traveling Highway 20 had a distinct advantage over the railroad — they could deliver goods to their customers' front doors.[14] Eventually passenger service was dropped, and the line concentrated on freight. In 1932, the railroad station at Yaquina was closed permanently.[15]

The Highway 20 of the 1920s (then known as Highway 26) met the needs of motorists for about a decade or so. Its safety came into question as traffic increased with newer cars that were engineered to travel at faster speeds. The accident rate on this route grew with each passing year.

Perhaps to give Highway 26 the appearance of a viable route worthy of upgrading, a movement began to have it officially designated as part of Highway 20. This route crossed the United States from Boston,

Massachusetts, to Albany, Oregon.[16] Several groups lobbied for the terminus of Highway 20 to be moved from Albany to Newport. In 1943, Lincoln County's state representative, "Shoeless" Joe Wilson (1895-1963), introduced legislation to designate Newport the official end of Highway 20. Wilson was known as "Shoeless" because he often took his shoes off in the state house, saying the thick carpet made his feet too hot. Just a few months after Wilson's legislative efforts, the Highway 20 designation was approved by the American Association of Highway Officials.[17] Newport became the terminus of the longest highway in the United States at that time.

Except for the installation of signs and the revision of road maps, not much changed after the official Highway 20 designation until a group of citizens formed the Oregon U.S. Highway 20 Association in 1947.[18] Its objective was to lobby for funds to rebuild the dangerous curves and "mediocre" construction of the 1920s.

Above: A sign photographed in 1959 declares Highway 20 "the Central Oregon route."

Left: The Oregon U.S. Highway 20 Association, which published this brochure, was formed in 1947 to lobby for safety improvements to the highway.

In 1952, construction began on the Toledo-Newport stretch to take out some of its 100 curves. When it was complete, this stretch was shortened from eight to six miles.

One of the worst sections was said to be the Newport-Toledo stretch. In 1948, advocates for straightening U.S. Highway 20 counted no fewer than 100 curves on this eight-mile "torturous trail." They lobbied the Legislature for funds to make year-round travel safer. Motorists grew weary of the dangerous curves. No longer did they want to continue "driving two miles to go one."[19]

Their efforts were not in vain. In 1952, the state provided $1.5 million to build four bridges and a new route just south of the old route.[20] After several seasons of road improvements and straightening in the 1950s, the

Newport-to-Toledo distance was shortened from eight to six miles.

In 1957, construction began on a cutoff road connecting Newport's Bayfront with the newly paved and widened Highway 20. It was named after the man who donated the land for its right of way, John Moore.[21] In 1958, construction began on a new route over Pioneer Mountain, and much of Highway 20 was repaved and widened. After a labor strike and several other delays, a new and improved Highway 20 opened in October 1960.[22] The Highway 20 Association then shifted its efforts away from lobbying for improvements to promoting the route. It published brochures and other promotional material encouraging motorists to "Take 20."

Despite all the construction work on Highway 20 during the 1950s, it became clear there was still room for improvement. In the 1960s, a Highway 20 upgrade, contemplated since 1928, came to fruition. A new route was constructed around the steep grades and sharp curves that plagued Toledo's city center.[23] As the bypass neared completion in late

In 1958, a new route was started over Pioneer Mountain and much of Highway 20 was repaved and widened. This photo was taken in 1959. (Lincoln County Leader)

1966, it was described as a "beautiful winding drive through wooded hillsides."[24]

With more than 130 years of paving, rerouting, and other improvements, Highway 20 steadily has become a faster and safer route. Upgrades usually have been slow in coming; the hilly terrain between Newport and the Willamette Valley makes improvements costly. This route has never been as fast or as safe as its travelers would like it to be. In 1885, it was described as "next to impassable for all practical purposes";[25] in the 1940s as a "torturous trail";[26] and in the 1960s as a "bottleneck."[27] Just prior to a major realignment between Cline Hill and Eddyville in the late 1990s, Highway 20 was described by an Oregon Department of Transportation official as "an older design" that "wouldn't be built that way today."[28]

Making this route safer and faster remains a priority with people living on the coast. The livelihood of many Lincoln County inhabitants depends directly or indirectly on transporting goods or people between the coast and the Willamette Valley. Safe travel on this route also enhances the lives of coastal residents who desire an occasional visit inland to take advantages of city life.

END NOTES
1. David F. Fagan, *History of Benton County, Oregon* (Portland: A.G. Walling, Printer, 1885), 478-480.
2. Evelyn Parry, *On Yaquina and the Big Elk* (Newport: Lincoln County Historical Society, 1985), 39.
3. Fagan, 480-481.
4. "Corvallis and Yaquina Bay Wagon Road," *Corvallis Gazette*, 12 March 1880.
5. "First Trip of 1913 to Newport," *Yaquina Bay News*, 03 July 1913.

6. Carlos A. Schwantes, *The Pacific Northwest: An Interpretive History* (Lincoln: University of Nebraska Press, 1989), 291.

7. Western Oregon U.S. Highway 20 Association, "Brief Presentation to the Legislative Interim Committee, April 13, 1948," in Oregon Coast History Center Archives.

8. "Highway Work Agreed Upon," *Yaquina Bay News*, 12 June 1919.

9. Schwantes, 292.

10. "Elk City Wants Highway," *Yaquina Bay News*, 3 July 1919.

11. "Auto Stage to Valley Inaugurated," *Yaquina Bay News*, 26 May 1921.

12. "Auto Bus Line from Newport to Corvallis and Albany," *Yaquina Bay News*, 09 June 1921.

13. Richard L. Price, *Newport, Oregon, 1866-1936: Portrait of a Coast Resort* (Newport: Lincoln County Historical Society, 1975), 83.

14. "Reducing Railroad Service," *Yaquina Bay News*, 29 Aug. 1928.

15. "Yaquina Passes as Railroad Station," *Yaquina Bay News*, 25 Feb. 1932.

16. "Highway 20 Looms in the Offing as a Certainty," *Yaquina Bay News*, 29 April 1943.

17. "National Highway No. 20 Ends at Newport," *Yaquina Bay News*, 20 May 1943.

18. "US 20 Meeting is at Corvallis C.C.," *Yaquina Bay News*, 20 Nov. 1947.

19. Western Oregon U.S. Highway 20 Association.

20. Untitled, *Lincoln County Leader*, 18 Sept. 1952.

21. "John Moore Donates Right-of-Way to Lincoln County for New Road," *The Newport News*, 06 Aug. 1957.

22. "Highway 20 Pioneer Road Open Monday," *The Newport News*, 20 Oct. 1960.

23. "Highway May Change Route," *Newport Journal*, 22 Feb. 1928.

24. "Paving Starts Soon on Toledo By-Pass," *News-Times*, 20 Oct. 1966.

25. Untitled, *Corvallis Gazette*, 03 April 1885.

26. Western Oregon U.S. Highway 20 Association.

27. "Lets Make It Really 'Highway' 20," *News-Times*, 31 March 1966.

28. Jamie Lerma, "ODOT Study Shows High Accident Rate on Highway 20," *News-Times*, 17 March 1994.

This section of Highway 20 into Toledo was bypassed eleven years after this photo was taken in August 1955.
(Lincoln County Leader)

OVER HERE

THE LINCOLN COUNTY HOME FRONT

Over there, over there
Send the word, send the word
Over there
That the Yanks are coming . . .

These song lyrics captured the patriotic enthusiasm that took hold in America when it entered into the war to end all wars, World War I. While most of the troops were sent to fight in Europe, several thousand Yanks were dispatched over here -- to Lincoln County. Personal stories reveal this friendly military invasion changed the central Oregon Coast and its people forever. In just a few short months, the war brought this region into the modern age.

Because the local papers reported on events overseas, just about everyone knew about the war in Europe. A large percentage of Lincoln County residents probably followed the war closely, as many of them were recent immigrants from Europe. Few may have suspected it would ever directly impact Lincoln County; after all, in 1914 the United States had issued a formal proclamation of neutral-

Opposite: Thanks to vast stands of strong, lightweight spruce ideal for biplanes, Lincoln County became a production center for the United States government during World War I. This trestle, north of Newport, was constructed to provide access to the spruce trees the government needed.

ity. But events in Europe led President Woodrow Wilson to proclaim a state of war with Germany in April 1917. A nationwide holiday was declared June 5, 1917. On this day, every man between the ages of twenty-one and thirty was required to register for a military draft.[1]

Six months later, word was received by Mr. and Mrs. R.A. Abbey of Elk City that their son, Alden, died of pneumonia while in service of his country in France. Alden Abbey was believed to be the first World War I casualty from Lincoln County.[2]

Not everyone in the service went overseas. Shortly after the United States entered the war, a special military division was created called the Spruce Production Division. Its goal: to boost the nation's production of Sitka spruce lumber from three to ten million board feet a year. Straight grain spruce is both strong and lightweight, ideal for construction of airplanes. Biplanes with a spruce framework were considered cutting-edge technology and vital to the war effort. The government felt the private sector could not possibly increase production fast enough to meet its needs. This was an era of bitter and sometimes violent labor unrest and strikes by the International Workers of the World ("The Wobblies") and others.[3] The head of the Spruce Division, Col. Brice P. Disque, put out a general call for data on the availability of standing Sitka spruce timber.[4] Lincoln County and four other areas in Oregon and Washington answered in a big way.

When information about the vast spruce stands in

Lincoln County was confirmed, life in the area quickened. In February, an advance team of about fifty men arrived and quietly went about planning construction of railroad lines from South Beach to the timber stands between the Alsea and Yachats rivers (estimated at a billion board feet); lines north from Newport to Spencer Creek; a huge sawmill in Toledo; and countless other projects. They set up a field camp at Beaver Lake and secured the Abbey Building on the Bayfront for their administrative offices. The ladies' restroom on Front and Case streets was used as a drafting room. It was announced that in a few weeks, 500 to 700 men would be arriving in the area.[5] Before war's end, more than 3,000 soldiers (many from the Midwest) and civilian employees went to work building whatever

Once Spruce Division soldiers arrived in Lincoln County, life in the area quickened. Buildings on the Bayfront were secured for administrative offices and a drafting room.
(Kinsey)

Cut-up plant under constru[...]
Toledo. Ore.

Toledo mill under construction, 1918. Thanks to World War I and the United States government, Toledo became home to one of the largest spruce mills in the world. (Kinsey)

was necessary to secure spruce for the war. While their time in the area was brief (less than a year), their impact was substantial — before the war, Lincoln County had less than 6,000 residents.

Who were these men and what were their stories? The archives at the Oregon Coast History Center contain information on a few of the soldiers who suddenly found themselves about as far west as you can go without getting on a boat.

One such soldier was Elmer Karpe (pronounced Car-PAY), originally from Minnesota. The son of a German immigrant, Karpe enlisted hoping to be shipped out to fight on the front lines. Because of his poor eyesight, he was rejected for this duty. Determined to help with the war effort anyway, he lied about his occupation and told the draft board he was a millwright. In fact, Karpe was a schoolteacher who was raised on a farm. A typewritten copy of his diary reveals he traveled to Toledo via troop train to work on construction of the mill. He arrived on August 7, 1918. He described Toledo as "a delightful pocket surrounded by hills covered with fir trees." During his first day on the job, he narrowly escaped death when a guy pole fell nearby. The next night he woke up in a sweat over the heights he had to conquer to place some braces. He wrote, "I'll never be fearless in the air." A few days later Karpe added, "I can't stand forty feet above the ground and walk on a twelve-inch cap and not feel shaky."

Karpe got a break from the heights when crews were laid off due to a shortage of milled lumber. Karpe passed the time at a Toledo recreation club, the YMCA, teaching illiterates to read, and by taking trips to Newport. A shortage of lumber must not have been the only example of managerial difficulties in the Spruce Division. Karpe noted in his diary, "More foolish red tape caused by poor management." To his own surprise, Karpe was rated among the ten best carpenters and worked on a crew building the rafters and flooring in the mill.

According to Karpe's diary, the spruce workers heard a rumor the war was over on November 8, 1918, and a celebration began only to be quashed when they were told it was untrue. Then on November 11, the men were awakened by blowing whistles; immediately they knew the war was over. "Our question at once was: When will we be dismissed?" Karpe wrote. At this point the mill was far from complet-

Bud "Buddy" Emery, in front of the fireplace at the Nye Beach restroom, 1916. In 1918, during his first year in school, the talented Emery would sing favorite wartime songs for the soldiers, who showered him with pennies, nickels, and even dimes in appreciation.

ed. Karpe said of the sentiment among his co-workers, "Men do not enjoy this life. They endured it as long as the need was there and the country was in grave danger. Now that the war is over they want to be out and away, especially not construction work, which they feel will only benefit the corporation." This was one of Karpe's last diary entries. It appears the men were dismissed in short order. By December 5, Elmer Karpe was in Thompson Falls, Montana, marrying the girl he had left behind when he became a part of the war effort. They raised four children

A Spruce Division camp at Agate Beach, 1918.

in Bakersfield, California.[6]

One child who experienced the presence of the spruce soldiers in Lincoln County was Newport resident Bud Emery, who recalled his wartime years in a 1997 autobiography. In the fall of 1918, Emery had just started his first year of school. Emery recalls a camp was located north of Newport at Agate Beach. Each weekend, entertainment-starved soldiers with passes would head to Newport. "Apparently the army did not like beach driving, as they constructed a system of wooden tracks from their camp to Newport for their trucks and vehicles to run on."

When one of these trucks rolled into town, Emery had both a potential stage and audience. The soldiers knew Emery was a talented singer and would lift the boy up on top of a truck, where he would "belt out the songs at the top of his voice." He quickly learned which wartime songs they liked: "K-K-K Katy," "How Ya Gonna Keep 'Em Down on the Farm," "Oh How I Hate To Get Up in the Morning," and others. While singing, he enjoyed a shower of pennies, nickels, and even dimes from the appreciative soldiers. This provided Emery with enough money for a trip to the skating rink and a candy bar or two. Perhaps more rewarding to the child was an occasional tear from a soldier's eye when Emery sang sentimental favorites, "Beautiful Dreamer," "I'm Forever Blowing Bubbles," and "Beautiful Ohio."[7]

German immigrant Fred C. Buehling, who worked as a civilian baker for the army in Toledo. Here he tries on a buddy's uniform for size, 1918.

German immigrant Fred C. Buehling never kept a diary or wrote of his experiences, but he did tell his son a little bit about his service in Toledo. As a young man, Buehling ran away to sea to be an apprentice baker. He traveled the world in that line of work and was once offered a bakery in Cape Town, South Africa. Buehling's son, Fred Jr., wrote in a letter to the Historical Society that he always wondered how his father ended up in Toledo.

"The Army had a civilian German baker . . . his accent was so thick he was sometimes difficult to understand." When the war was over, Buehling was offered a bakery in Toledo, "but he turned it down, probably because he'd had enough of the deep woods."[8]

The woods at South Beach (across Yaquina Bay from Newport) were also the scene of a boom in activity. Idaho Point (then called Hinton's Point, before that Point Virtue) was chosen as the beginning of the railroad line that headed south to Yachats. In April, the local newspaper reported on the arrival of one hundred men at South Beach.

Warren Spruce Company mess hall, 1918. (Prentiss)

145

*Spruce Division
soldiers relax on the
dock at South
Beach, 1918.*

"Uncle Sam's Boys are working like beavers to establish their camp so they can get to work on the new railroad."[9] Delbert Pruner (1909-1982), whose family had a ranch on Theil Creek, recalled that when the Spruce Division left South Beach, "They dug huge pits burying all their produce and stuff, bacon, cans of lard." Locals salvaged several hundred pounds of discarded food and put it to good use.[10]

A temporary hospital was also set up at South Beach (about where the intersection of Highway 101 and Anchor Way is now) for the soldiers who contracted the flu. A life-threatening strain of the flu swept through the country in 1918. Quarantines were placed on the spruce camps at the height of the epidemic. A second hospital was established at Nye Beach in the Kelly Hotel (on what is now West Third Street). The hotel was completely remodeled to include an operating room — a first for Newport.[11]

Construction of the countless buildings and railroad lines was done in extreme haste; the one and only goal of the Spruce Division was to boost spruce production for the war effort. Efficiency and government waste were issues given little thought during this wartime operation. The Spruce Division was a complex bureaucracy that was neither purely military nor purely civilian. During its first few months of existence, it was reorganized several times; finally the Spruce Production Division ended up as part of the Air Service. The soldiers, who were paid military wages, were actually employed by private contractors such as the Warren Spruce Company. The Spruce Division contracts with private logging companies were all on a cost-plus basis.[12]

It is not known how many jobs were created for Lincoln County residents, but without a doubt the influx of more than 3,000 men created many employment opportu-

This hospital at South Beach was for soldiers who had contracted a life-threatening strain of the flu. Quarantines were placed on the spruce camps at the height of the epidemic.

nities for locals.

Volunteer opportunities also were created. Red Cross chapters and several YMCAs sprung up near many of the larger Spruce Division camps. The YMCAs provided wholesome entertainment and enrichment for the soldiers. The Knights of Columbus assembled a Bayfront reading room for the incoming soldiers inside the opera house on First Street. At the conclusion of the war, a library association formed to manage the books and maintain a library. This marked the beginning of the Newport Public Library.[13]

Perhaps one of the more unusual calls for volunteers was issued by the Red Cross for sphagnum moss pickers. This type of moss, commonly called bog moss, was said to grow in the wetland areas of the forest. Highly absorbent, it was used by the Red Cross as a substitute for cotton. Two bogs with sphagnum moss were known to exist in Lincoln County: one at Beaver Creek, the other, known as the "Priest Bog," at South Beach. The call for volunteers in the local paper pleaded, "when you realize how the unusual economic activities have tied up the working power of this region, will not every one respond gladly and loyally and use the opportunity to do their bit."[14]

The soldiers also "did their bit" during their nine-month stay in Lincoln County. Thanks to the work completed by the Spruce Production Division, the infrastructure for a major wood products industry was in place. The soldiers completed more than forty miles of railroad track. Tracks were laid from Toledo into the Siletz Valley, from

Yaquina City north to Spencer Creek. The longest stretch of track ran south from South Beach, across the Alsea Bay and through Waldport to just north of Yachats. The soldiers also nearly completed the largest spruce mill in the world in Toledo. At the end of the war, all of the Spruce Production Division railroad lines, the Toledo mill, and timber holdings were placed on the auction block.

It would be a little while before Lincoln County would benefit fully from the efforts of the Spruce Production Division. After war's end, the railroad lines saw little use. The route south was used to transport passengers and mail to Waldport in 1920. This line and the big

Spruce Division workers completed more than forty miles of railroad track, reaching from Toledo into the Siletz Valley, from Yaquina City north to Spencer Creek, and from South Beach to just north of Yachats. This picture was taken October 1, 1918.
(Prentiss)

mill in Toledo and the large forest known as the Blodgett Tract were purchased for $2 million by the Pacific Spruce Corporation, later known as C.D. Johnson Co.[15] The mill was not completed and running at capacity until 1923. The railroad line known as the Yaquina Northern, which ran to the small sawmill at Otter Rock, was purchased by the Multnomah Lumber and Box Company in 1921. In 1923, the roundhouse and machine shop on this line at Moolack Creek burned to the ground.[16] The venture did not endure as long as the C.D. Johnson Company (which was bought out by Georgia-Pacific in 1951). Apparently the Box Company's railroad and timber lands reverted to the Spruce Production Division. In 1929, the Atlantic Western Company began negotiating with this agency for the purchase of Yaquina Northern. It also talked with the Port of Newport about leasing McLean Point to establish a staging area for assembling ocean-going log rafts.[17]

For a few short months in 1918, Lincoln County was a staging area for aircraft production. The perceived need for straight-grain Sitka spruce lumber for the war in Europe changed Lincoln County forever. Railroad tracks, hospitals, sawmills, roads, and countless other improvements were hurried along at an incredible pace. For Lincoln County, it was the beginning of a new economic era -- one based on a full-scale wood products industry.

Many historians perceive World War I as the end of American isolation from world events. Lincoln County learned for the first time that events in distant Europe could change the local economy and day-to-day living almost overnight. It is fortunate that a few stories about this area's sudden entry into the modern age have been preserved.

END NOTES
1. "War Census Day Facts," *Yaquina Bay News*, 31 May 1917.
2. "First Lincoln County Boy Dies In France," *Yaquina Bay News*, 17 Jan. 1918.
3. Brigadier General Brice P. Disque, *History of Spruce Production Division*, self published circa 1920, Oregon Coast History Center Archives #85.116.7, pgs. 15-16.
4. "Government Wants Spruce Information," *Yaquina Bay News*, 27 Dec. 1917.
5. "Government Gets Lincoln County Spruce," *Yaquina Bay News*, 07 Feb. 1918.
6. Elmer Karpe, "Diary of Elmer Karpe,"OCHC Archives, #95.39.
7. Bud Emery, "Jefferies/Emery Family History Chapter III," 1997, OCHC Archives, "Jefferies" biography file.
8. Fred C. Buehling to author, July 1997, OCHC "Buehling" biography file.
9. Untitled, *Yaquina Bay News*, 25 April 1918.
10. Delbert Pruner, interviewer unknown, 1978, transcribed tape recording, OCHC archives, Newport.
11. "Newport has a Hospital," *Yaquina Bay News*, 27 June 1918.
12. Disque, pgs. 9-36.
13. Harriet Daugherty, "Gives History of Library," *Newport Journal*, 07 Feb. 1940.
14. "Sphagnum Moss," *Yaquina Bay News*, 18 July 1918.
15. *Pacific Spruce Corporation and its Subsidiaries*, ed., Bolling Arthur Johnson (Newport: C.D. Johnson Co., 1924, Lincoln County Historical Society, 1996), 16.
16. Lloyd Palmer, *Steam Towards the Sunset* (Newport: Lincoln County Historical Society, 1990), 159-162.
17. "Logging Will Start in Short Time," *Yaquina Bay News*, 13 Feb. 1929.

Spruce Division soldiers take a gander at sunbathers on Nye Beach, 1918.

The New Cliff House,
1921. It reportedly was
traded to Peter and
Cecile Gilmore for their
chicken ranch.

SYLVIA BEACH HOTEL
IF ONLY THOSE WALLS COULD TALK...

A pool, jacuzzi, cable television, and an extra phone line for internet access are all features desired by many in a modern motel. The Sylvia Beach Hotel in Nye Beach has none of these. But it does offer amenities increasingly sought after in these hectic times: conversation, contemplation, and something of substance to read that is not on a computer terminal.

The Sylvia Beach Hotel itself is a substantive tale of fascinating history, a place where the saying, "If only those walls could talk," is especially apropos.

The Sylvia Beach began as Wilson D. Wheeler's New Cliff House Hotel. Like well-known Nye Beach photographer and agate jeweler A.L. Thomas, Wheeler came from the Waldo Hills area of Salem. Before coming to the coast, Wheeler ran a meat market and did some farming.[1] Wheeler left Salem for Newport in October 1909 to purchase the Cliff House property next-door to the hot sea baths in Nye Beach.[2] A 1910 Sanborn map reveals the

Bathing beauties such as these were popular sights at Nye Beach in front of the Gilmore.

old Cliff House property contained a fair-sized house, probably used as a boarding house, and a couple of large tents. Tent camping in Nye Beach was quite popular at that time.

In 1910, Wheeler began construction of a new hotel called the New Cliff House on this property. It is not known when Wheeler took in his first registered guest, but nearly three years after the ground-breaking, the framing work for the third story was just starting.[3] Wheeler was known as a thrifty businessman whose reputation as a hotel manager brought guests to the New Cliff House from nearly every state in the Union.[4]

According to one account, by 1921 Wheeler had grown tired of running the hotel and traded it to Peter and Cecile Gilmore for their chicken ranch just outside of town. The Gilmores had lived in Newport since 1917.[5] In addition to the chicken ranch, the Gilmores also ran a dry goods store.[6]

Renamed the Gilmore Hotel, it continued to thrive under its new owners. It lay in the heart of Nye Beach, the recreation center of the central Oregon Coast. Next-door was Dr. Minthorn's Hot Sea Baths, which since 1900 had drawn health seekers who believed soaking in heated seawater would help cure a long list of ailments.[7] Next to the sea baths was the Natatorium, home of a large saltwater swimming pool, dance floor, roller skating rink, and a variety of other ever-changing amusements. The Natatorium was located where the turnaround parking lot is today.

Nye Beach also offered small nickelodeon theaters, shooting galleries, gift shops, and bowling alleys -- not to mention the biggest attractions of all, the ocean and a nice sandy beach.

The Gilmores arranged for their hotel to become a stop for a seven-passenger Studebaker car that shuttled tourists twice daily from Corvallis.[8] Their own car transported passengers to the hotel who had arrived via the ferry on the Bayfront.

With the tourism industry prospering, the Gilmores began positioning themselves to expand their operation. In 1928, Cecile Gilmore's mother, Sarah Irvin, who at one time ran a millinery store in Newport, purchased a hotel just north of the Natatorium called the Ocean View (originally known as the Nicolai).[9] She spent three months redecorat-

Nye Beach, 1910s. The New Cliff House (second from the right) sat next-door to a favorite Nye Beach amusement, Dr. Minthorn's Hot Sea Baths. The Ocean View Hotel is at extreme left.

155

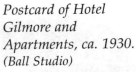
Postcard of Hotel Gilmore and Apartments, ca. 1930. (Ball Studio)

ing the place before reopening.[10]

That same year, Peter and Cecile purchased the late Dr. Minthorn's sea baths. The Gilmores now owned 125 feet of ocean property along Nye Beach. Peter announced his plans to move the sea baths into the basement of the building and tear down its upper floors. He also declared his intention to build a first-class modern hotel on the site as soon as he could arrange financing.[11]

All this was not to be. Five months later, Peter was killed in an auto accident while driving along Highway 20 with Cecile and their dog, Pat. They were headed on the downhill side of Pioneer Mountain toward Corvallis when they hit ice, skidded, and rolled over. Peter was killed instantly; his wife was pinned under the car. Pat took off running back to some construction workers they had passed earlier. The canine barked as loud as he could, but the workers ignored him. Finally Pat grabbed the pant leg of one of the workers with his teeth and pulled him in the direction of the wreck. The other workers followed to find Cecile Gilmore still alive. The crew went to work lifting the car to free her.

Pat had earned a statewide reputation for his incredible intelligence and amazing tricks long before the car wreck. He acted as the Gilmore Hotel's bellhop and messenger, running errands for his master from the basement to the attic. He also was the official mail carrier, delivering letters to the guests in their rooms. Oftentimes the canine's tricks were the evening's entertainment.[12]

Both Pat and Cecile recovered from the wreck, but without a doubt their lives changed dra-

Postcard from the Hotel Gilmore, 1920s.

Pat, the heroic canine of the Gilmore, poised on the fender of the hotel car, ca. 1925. Pat was the hotel's bellhop and popular entertainment for the guests.

matically. Peter's plans for the first-class hotel were never realized. The old sea bath building was used as apartments managed by Cecile for years. Eventually it was torn down and the Yaquina Art Center was built on this site.

The loss of her husband probably was not the only factor that prevented Cecile from developing the sea bath property; less than a year after Peter's death, the nation entered an economic depression. Tourism slowed through the depression years and did not rebound completely until the mid-1940s, after the end of World War II.

By that time, Cecile was more than sixty years old. She sold out in 1957 to Donald Young, who also owned a small chain of lumber yards called Oregon-Willamette Lumber Company. Young announced his plans to put a restaurant in the hotel.[13] Five years later, it was purchased by Bill Robinson who stated in an interview, "in 1967 it was an empty, desolate building."[14] Robinson reopened with a bang, throwing a Halloween open house in which he invited the entire town. Two to three hundred people accepted his invitation, forcing him to start closing the packed hotel. He started at the top floor and worked his way down. The party was not manageable until he closed everything but the bottom floor. After the opening, Robinson ran the Gilmore as an apartment building with rooms costing forty to fifty dollars a month. Perhaps the most accurate description of the Gilmore at this point was written on one of its bathroom walls: "The only flophouse on the West Coast with an ocean view and a waiting list to get in."[15] Low rent and the beautiful setting of the Gilmore attracted a diverse group of people, including artists, musicians, motel maids, a nurse, fish plant workers, bartenders, and laundry work-

The Gilmores purchased Dr. Minthorn's Hot Sea Baths in 1928 and converted the building into apartments. This site is now home to the Yaquina Art Center.

ers, to name a few. One resident, Ed Cameron, moved into the Gilmore in 1979 and began publishing the *Gilmore Gazette*, which featured local poets, artists, and comics. "Basically what the *Gazette* did was print anything that anybody wanted," Cameron said in a 1994 interview.[16]

The eclectic Gilmore residents banded together in June 1984 when the hotel was sold and they were served with thirty-day eviction notices. The "Gilmore Tenants Association" retained a legal-aid attorney to fight the loss of their affordable housing.[17] Their efforts were unsuccessful, but four residents refused to leave: James DeNord, Patrick Duffy, Gregory Kern, and Sandra Bunce. A month after the eviction notice was served, James DeNord, the last of the four holdouts, checked out of the dilapidated Gilmore.[18]

The new owners, Goody Cable and Sally Ford, announced plans to completely renovate the Gilmore. While the outer appearance was retained, the interior was

The Gilmore Hotel, 1940s. Cecile Gilmore continued to operate the hotel for many years after her husband's death.

The Gilmore,
October 1,
1981.
(Roger A.
Hart)

completely redone to cater to book lovers. Each of the twenty guest rooms was redecorated in the theme of a different author.[19] The Gilmore was rechristened the Sylvia Beach Hotel after Sylvia Beach, one of the century's greatest patrons of literature. Authors such as F. Scott Fitzgerald, Ernest Hemingway, and James Joyce hung out at her Paris bookstore, Shakespeare and Co.

As anyone familiar with remodeling knows, it is not easy and things seldom go according to plan. Some of the partners in the project did not share the same vision for the hotel. The plumbing and wiring were shot. The back of the building had to be jacked up to reinforce the structure and concrete footings had to be poured. About one hundred twenty yards of debris had to be removed from the hotel. Financing for the project experienced delays. But Cable and Ford's perseverance paid off: the Sylvia Beach Hotel finally opened in 1987.

During the years when the Sylvia Beach sat vacant and in transition, the Nye Beach area began a transition as well. Art galleries and other new businesses began to spring up, and plans were made for a new performing arts center.

Peter Gilmore may not have seen his dream of a "first-class modern hotel" come true; but his vision did become reality with the opening of the Sylvia Beach, though the first-class hotel might be considered more anti-modern than modern. Visitors will not find a jacuzzi or a pool, and none of the rooms have a television or a telephone. What visitors will find are books everywhere, a great restaurant that serves dinner family-style, and an atmosphere that lends itself to conversation, contemplation, and reading -- the old-fashioned way.

END NOTES
1. "W.D. Wheeler Dies in Salem at Daughter's House," *Yaquina Bay News*, 11 Aug. 1940.
2. "Local Notes," *Yaquina Bay News*, 21 Oct. 1921.
3. "Local Notes," 27 Feb. 1913.
4. "W.D. Wheeler Dies."
5. "P.G. Gilmore Dies in Auto Accident," *Yaquina Bay News*, 10 Jan. 1929.
6. "Young Buys Local Hotel Near Beach," *Newport News*, 1957.
7. "The Hot Sea Baths, Nye Beach, Newport, Ore.," *Yaquina Bay News-Reporter*, 7 July 1910.
8. "Auto Bus Line From Newport to Corvallis and Albany," *Yaquina Bay News*, 9 June 1921.
9. "Ocean View Hotel Sold," *Yaquina Bay News*, 16 Feb. 1928.
10. "Ocean View Hotel Now Open," *Yaquina Bay News*, 17 May 1928.
11. "Buys Hot Sea Baths," *Newport Journal*, 22 Aug. 1928.
12. "Gilmore Hotel Mourns Death of Pat, Old Canine Servant," *Yaquina Bay News*, 25 April 1935.
13. "Young Buys Local Hotel."
14. Dennis Curran, "The Gilmore By the Sea," *Inkfish*, July 1994, 3.
15. Ibid, 3.
16. Ibid, 3-4.
17. Lisa Mihnos, "Remodeling Plans Back on Front Burner," *Newport News-Times*, 29 March 1986.
18. Duane Honsowetz, "Last Man Leaves Gilmore," *Statesman-Journal*, 4 Aug. 1984.
19. "Gilmore Restoration Effort Taking Shape," *Newport News-Times,* 12 Sept. 1984.

"THE ABBEY," NEWPORT, ORE.

WHEN THE COAST WAS DRY

THE ABBEY RAID

At 11:00 a.m., Sept. 14, 1923, a team of twenty deputies, local police, and "secret service men" quietly surrounded Newport's largest and most prominent Bayfront establishment. No one, not even the citizenry walking past, was aware of what was about to take place. State Prohibition Officer George L. Cleaver gave the order for the men to close in; the warrant was read and the search for the contraband of the day -- liquor — was under way. This was the largest liquor raid ever held in Lincoln County. The place: the famous Abbey Hotel.[1]

Originally called the Bay View, the Abbey Hotel was established in 1867[2] by Canadians Peter and Cerena Abbey.[3] Over the years, the Abbey (in its various Bayfront locations) enjoyed a sterling reputation as the place that accommodated the rich and poor alike. "Mother" Abbey's cooking was famous statewide. One reporter remembered fondly that it " 'didn't matter if you had a nickel or not,' mother Abbey would say, 'I've got the best clams ever and

Opposite: The Abbey Hotel formally opened on May 27, 1911. Twelve years later, it was the scene of the biggest liquor raid ever in Lincoln County.

hot biscuits and some real huckleberry pie -- right in there to wash yourself up and you just go right in and sit up to the table and the girls will look after you.' "[4]

Cerena Abbey, ca. 1910. The man next to her is probably her husband, Peter. The Abbeys started their hotel business in Newport in 1867. Cerena was known for her hospitality and huckleberry pie. (Castle Studio)

But this was a new era, the roaring 1920s, Newport style. Management of the Abbey had passed to Ed and Mort Abbey, Peter and Cerena's sons. The brothers had assisted their parents in getting the huge three-story structure built in 1910-11, and they assumed ownership after their parents died in 1916.[6]

When the Prohibition officers made their way to the chicken coop behind the hotel that September morning, they found a still. They also seized as evidence jugs, bottles, kegs, and five "recently filled" bottles of whiskey. Two registered guests and Hop Gee, the hotel's laundry man, were arrested. The Abbey brothers also were placed under arrest.[7] The raid received thorough front-page coverage in the Newport newspaper, *Yaquina Bay News*. One of the deputies participating in the raid was the paper's editor, William Mathews, a strong supporter of Prohibition. Mathews always found room on the front page to publicize

166

who was arrested for Prohibition violations and to expound the evils of drink. When the Abbey case came to trial, the defense attorneys for the Abbeys alleged Mathews had abused them in his newspaper. Mathews countered that the Abbeys had threatened him with violence.[8]

Once the raid at the Abbey was in progress, other units of policemen were dispatched all over the county. Newport's "Midget Restaurant" was raided, and about half a dozen Bayfront regulars were rounded up. Three men at a logging camp of the Multnomah Lumber and Box Company were arrested for selling liquor. A pool hall was busted for gambling activities. The officers headed to Toledo, where they made a few more arrests. The only real trouble officers encountered took place in Burnt Woods, farther east. One of the police cars collided with another car. No one was hurt, but the officers' car would not be

Cerena and her staff in the Abbey lobby, ca. 1912. The Abbey enjoyed a sterling reputation statewide as an establishment that catered to rich and poor alike.

going anywhere until repairs were made. They were forced to leave the car overnight at the local garage. When deputies returned the following day to check with the mechanic, they were no doubt shocked to discover "their car stripped of every removable part."[9] Whether the culprit was ever caught is not known.

While most of those arrested pleaded guilty and paid their fines, the Abbey trial became the stuff of newspaper headlines. The brothers faced charges of maintaining a common nuisance, possession of a still, and illegal possession of narcotics. At the trial, Cleaver, the sheriff, Mathews, and a host of other law enforcement officials described the contraband discovered at the raid on the Abbey Hotel. One agent, William McMillis, testified that E.J. Abbey had personally sold him a quart of whiskey.

Abbey countered that when the whiskey was alleged to have been sold to McMillis, he was in Portland. He produced a witness and a hotel guest book with his sig-

Cerena and Peter's sons, Mort (above) and Ed, were arrested as a result of the liquor raid on the Abbey Hotel. They were later acquitted because of a lack of evidence. (Eastman)

168

nature for the very day he was alleged to have sold the booze in Newport. The defense attorneys for the Abbey brothers also produced a parade of upstanding members of the community who claimed to have visited the Abbey on countless occasions and never seen a still. The defense argued the Abbeys could not be responsible for the drinking activities of their guests and went on to claim that some of the contraband was planted during a second search. The still, the Abbeys argued, was found in an old building that had not been in use since Prohibition went into effect. The jury deliberated for fifty-five minutes and found the Abbeys innocent of all charges.

The state's case against the brothers probably was substantially weakened by a lack of physical evidence, thanks to mysterious figures in the night. After the raid, the

In front of the Abbey Hotel, late 1910s.

169

contraband had been locked up by the sheriff at the county jail in Toledo. A day or two later, unknown parties with a key entered the jail and destroyed most of what had been confiscated at the Abbey Hotel.[10]

The conclusion of the trial in August 1924 marked the beginning of the end of the Abbeys' involvement with the landmark hotel. Less than one year later, the place sold to John Tobin.[11] It may never be known for sure if the selling of the hotel had anything to do with the raid and subsequent trial. An article in the local paper written about a year later stated the Abbeys sold the hotel because of a "new kind of tourist": one who traveled by automobile and checked in for just a night or two before he was "off to another beach." Before the preponderance of autos, it was not uncommon for guests to stay at the Abbey for a month at a time during the summer.[12]

After selling the hotel, Ed Abbey remained involved in the operation of other hotels and restaurants on the West Coast, from Arizona to Alaska. He stayed in the hospitality industry for the remainder of his life and kept Newport as his base of operations. He died in 1937 at age seventy-one while staying at the Abbey Hotel. E.J. Abbey had no survivors.[13]

His brother, Mort, also remained in Newport and was a businessman with many interests. He was president of the Roosevelt Highway Ferry Co. and Newport Navigation Co. These two companies contracted with the state to run the ferries at Newport and Waldport. He also

This Abbey Hotel was torn down in 1910 to make way for a larger and more modern Abbey.

owned a cement plant and a fuel business and controlled the loading of lumber freighters in Yaquina Bay. Mort Abbey died in 1933 while staying at the Imperial Hotel in Portland. He had left Newport to negotiate with the State Highway Commission for a new ferry contract. He was survived by one daughter, who was living in Los Angeles.[14]

Long after the Abbeys had divested themselves of the hotel, their name continued to grace the building. John Tobin, who served as mayor of Newport for three terms, ran the Abbey for about eighteen years. Tobin sold it in 1942 to William A. Shane, who in turn sold it to Marvin Uhlenhake in partnership with his brother-in-law, Charles Havlicek, in 1949.[15] While doing some bulldozing work near the hotel, Uhlenhake's workers discovered something that may have been overlooked in the raid of 1923. "Hundreds of bottles of bootleg whiskey" and "a pipe that ran the illegal booze into the hotel's tavern" were unearthed.[16] In 1959, Uhlenhake sold the Abbey to its final owner, George Barr.[17] On May 10, 1964, at 1:05 a.m., a fire was reported at the Abbey. By the time the sun rose, the place had burned to the ground.[18]

Six of its ten tenants were rescued by the fire department.[19] It had one registered guest that night.[20] While three people were treated for smoke inhalation, no one was seriously hurt.[21] When the Abbey burned, it was long past its heyday; its glory days had come to an end in 1936 with the completion of the Yaquina Bay Bridge and the rerouting of Highway 101 away from the Bayfront.

A much smaller, "modern old English" structure named the Abbey Bar and Restaurant was built on the old hotel site in 1966. The new Abbey featured two bars, a

Interior of the Abbey, 1930s.

The Abbey Hotel,
ca. 1912.

restaurant, banquet room, and a dance floor equipped with an "advanced stereo discotheque system."[22] This has since been torn down to make way for parking spaces.[23]

Despite the demolition of the last of this series of establishments, the Abbey name lives on. Abbey Street and the Abbey Street Pier are reminders of the famous and infamous history of the Abbeys and their legendary Bayfront hotel. The name Abbey not only conjures up images of good food and lodging, but serves as a reminder of the Roaring 1920s, Newport style.

END NOTES
1. "Big Liquor Raid Staged," *Yaquina Bay News*, 20 Sept. 1923.
2. "The Abbey Hotel, P.M. Abbey, Proprietor," *Yaquina Bay News*,

11 Aug. 1904.

3. Lucy F. Blue, *A Glimpse of Newport 75 Years Ago* (Waldport: Mr. and Mrs. Paul Van De Velde, 1949), 3.

4. "Why Not be Sensible?", *Yaquina Bay News*, 15 April 1926.

5. "Spacious New Abbey House," *Newport Signal,* 02 March 1911.

6. Evelyn Parry, *At Rest In Lincoln County* (Newport: Lincoln County Historical Society, 1979), 45.

7. "Big Liquor Raid Staged," *Yaquina Bay News*, 20 Sept. 1923.

8. "Abbey Hotel Proprietors Acquitted By Jury," *Yaquina Bay News*, 24 Aug. 1924.

9. "Big Liquor Raid Staged."

10. "Abbey Hotel Proprietors Acquitted."

11. "The Abbey Hotel Changes Ownership," *Yaquina Bay News,* 02 April 1925.

12. "Why Not be Sensible?"

13. "Edwin Abbey Passes Away," *Newport Journal,* 14 April 1937.

14. "Mort Abbey Dies," clipping from unknown newspaper in OCHC biography file, probably from Portland, 1933.

15. Ray Moe, "Last Version of the Abbey Gives Way to Parking Lot," *Newport News-Times*, 19 Sept. 1984.

16. Lynn Jeffress, "Bayfront Memories: The Abbey Hotel," *The Bayfront*, July 1993.

The Abbey as it looked in the 1960s before it was destroyed by fire in 1964.

Above: The first Abbey Hotel (on the right), ca. 1907. (Charles Bradshaw)

Left: In early days, the arrival of the ferry on the Bayfront (ca. 1903) usually meant more customers for the Abbeys, who owned the hotel and a controlling interest in the ferry.

17. "Prominent Buildings Sold Here," *The Newport News*, 08 October 1959.
18. "Fire Razes Newport Landmark," *The Oregonian*, 11 May 1964.
19. Ibid.
20. Lynn Jeffress.
21. "Fire Razes Newport Landmark."
22. "New Abbey Opens," *News-Times*, 27 Jan. 1960.
23. Moe.

THE GREAT
DEBATE OF 1928

In the late 1920s, Prohibition and the presidential election were the issues making headlines in the nation's newspapers -- but not in Lincoln County. Local residents found themselves embroiled in the Great Debate of 1928, consisting of two key issues: placement of the new Roosevelt Highway (now Highway 101) and location of the county seat.

The underlying cause of the political upheaval was Lincoln County's entry into the automobile age. Up until the 1920s, tourists traveling to the central Oregon Coast stayed in Newport. Travel to the north or south of Newport was difficult if not impossible. In short, Newport had a monopoly on the tourist trade. But this was all about to change with the construction of the Roosevelt Military Highway.

The Great Debate began when the highway progressed as far south as Siletz Bay.[1] Toledo residents lobbied to route the highway up the Siletz River, through Toledo and across Yaquina River about where Butler Bridge is now. The highway would continue southward over the

Opposite: The old Lincoln County Courthouse, which was built in Toledo in 1899. This photo was taken in 1955, three years after Newport had finally wrestled the county seat from Toledo.
(Lincoln County Leader)

hills to Bayview, just across the Alsea River from Waldport.[2] Yet another plan called for the road to bypass Waldport completely.[3] When these proposals failed and final plans placed the highway straight down the coast from Siletz Bay to Newport, Toledo lobbied yet again to turn the coast highway inland to Toledo and through the hills to Waldport.[4]

Today these proposed inland routes may seem convoluted, but at the time they were not without merit. With 2,100 people -- twenty-one percent of the county's population --- Toledo was the largest town in Lincoln County. (Today Toledo comprises about eight percent). In the 1920s, the Pacific Spruce Corporation (C.D. Johnson) and several other sawmills were based in Toledo, creating the largest year-round payroll in the county. Toledo also was home to a cooperage, creamery, and the county seat. In short, Toledo was the place where folks lived, worked, shipped their wares, and ran the county government.

The Toledo plan also made some sense because the state announced, for budgetary reasons, it might require the county to finance free ferries across

Lincoln County Bank, Toledo, 1920s. In the 1920s, Toledo was the place where folks lived, worked, shipped their wares, and ran the county government.

each of the bays. The county did not have the funds to provide such a service, and Toledo already had a bridge across the Yaquina River.[5]

The second issue in the Great Debate -- whether to move the Lincoln County Courthouse from Toledo to Newport -- had everything and nothing to do with placement of the highway. In March 1928, a delegation met in Newport to discuss plans for launching a campaign to relocate the courthouse. Newspapers reported the sole topic of conversation was a protest filed by the Port of Toledo with the United States government against a proposed bridge across Yaquina Bay at Newport. The Port of Toledo contended the bridge would be a menace to navigation.[6] At this point, there is little to indicate the county seat removal movement was very serious. The meeting appears to have been an opportunity to vent.

After a state Highway Department public hearing

Toledo's bid to route the new Roosevelt Military Highway (Highway 101) through its town made some sense — Toledo already had built a bridge over the Yaquina River about where Butler Bridge is now. This photo was taken in June 1960. (Lincoln County Leader)

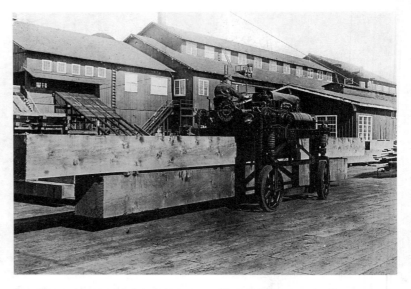

Pacific Spruce Corporation mill, 1920s. The mill opposed a bridge across the Yaquina River at Newport, fearing it would hinder the company's ability to tow log rafts upriver to the mill.

on the proposed highway south of Newport, the movement picked up steam yet again. The department had concluded the coast highway should end at the north side of Yaquina Bay in Newport and resume on the south side of the bay at South Beach. The hearing was to discuss the exact placement of the highway so when a bridge was built across the bay, the highway would not have to be rerouted. At this meeting, the proposed north end of the bridge was to be at McLean Point,[7] about where the Port of Newport international dock stands today.

No one, including the Port of Toledo, voiced any objections until a representative from the Pacific Spruce Corporation stood up and read an eight-page typed document outlining his company's objections to a bridge across Yaquina Bay. The Pacific Spruce Corporation felt a bridge would be a navigation hazard, making it difficult to tow log rafts upriver to its Toledo mill. Twelve other employees of the Spruce Corporation then submitted written protests, all supposedly very similar in substance.[8]

A week after this meeting, "The Newport For County Seat Club" took its first real steps toward removing the county seat from Toledo. They called a special election to approve the selling of $20,000 in bonds to finance an addition to the recently completed city hall building to house the county seat. The city would then allow the county to use the addition at no cost. Construction of the addition was contingent upon a favorable countywide vote to move the county seat to Newport.[9] An article appearing in the Toledo paper, the *Lincoln County Leader*, pointed out that Newport and Toledo first went to battle for the county seat shortly after Lincoln County's formation in 1893 and that, "Toledo would meet the issues at every turn . . . and the electors would decide the issue in the best interest of the county."[10]

*Courthouse in Toledo,
early 1900s.*

Bathers at Nye Beach, 1922. Thanks to the freedom of the automobile in the 1920s, fewer tourists spent the whole summer in Newport — causing residents to lobby hard for the county seat to help sustain the economy.

Things heated up a little when word reached Toledo that people in Newport were spreading rumors that the twenty-nine-year-old courthouse was in poor condition and had been condemned, and that Toledo had more than its share of schools. An editorial in the *Lincoln County Leader* detailed recent improvements to the courthouse building and countered, "a more central location could not be secured." This was made possible by a recently completed road from Siletz to Taft and "a six-mile connection south from the Toledo bridge" that made Beaver Creek and Drift Creek neighbors. The editorial also countered that Toledo had more schools because it was the largest town in Lincoln County.[11]

In August, Newport voters approved the selling of bonds for a courthouse addition to the city hall: 293 votes yes, 29 no.[12] Toledo then organized a committee to counter Newport's courthouse removal efforts.[13] Newport and Toledo found they were not the only towns in Lincoln County; Taft (now part of Lincoln City) wanted to be rec-

Cottages on Hurbert Street between Second and Olive streets, probably 1922. While Toledo experienced an economic boom and housing shortage, Newport suffered from a surplus of summer cottages that sat vacant in winter months.

ognized as a town with which to be reckoned. In a light-hearted article in the Taft newspaper, it was suggested its town would be the logical choice for a county seat. The pending road improvements were making north county a hub of activity. The Taft author realized the crux of the county seat issue really was the economic implications brought about by road improvements: "Newport's day has gone forever when she can no longer hold full control of the tourist business . . . her tourist monopoly is broken."[14]

Newport indeed was insecure about its future economic prospects. In the 1920s, Toledo experienced an economic boom that resulted in a housing shortage. Newport, on the other hand, had a surplus of tourist cabins and houses that sat empty during the winter months. Typically, cottage owners increased their rates in the summer. One newspaper editorial called for an end to this practice.

"Without a doubt, fifty new families could be induced to locate in Newport if they were assured that the rents would not be doubled on them during the summer months."[15] Increased use of the automobile was reshaping the economy. Passenger rail service to Yaquina Bay was being scaled back by the Southern Pacific Railroad.[16] The editor of the *Newport Journal* observed, "When the majority of the people of Newport realize that the average citizen of the Willamette Valley is not spending the entire summer at one beach resort, as in years gone by, but is now on the road every weekend," it will again enjoy a thriving tourist "crop."[17] Indeed, in the 1920s, towns with a tourist-based economy sprung up every few miles along the highway in north Lincoln County.

Newport soon found out that moving the courthouse was not the economic answer in this period of adjustment. In the November election, the county seat removal measure was soundly defeated: 2,272 no, 1,319 yes. Removal of the county seat would become an issue that Lincoln County would visit a total of five times[18] before it was finally approved in 1952.

Each attempt at moving the county seat had its own particular set of issues; in 1928 the underlying issue, aside from simple town rivalry, was how the economic pie was going to be re-sliced after road construction. New roads and very mobile tourists turned Lincoln County's economy on its end. In north county, new towns sprung up. In Newport and Toledo, residents experienced an economic anxiety attack that manifested itself in a battle for a highway and a courthouse. It would be some years before residents in all of Lincoln County reconciled themselves to their share of the new economic pie.

The new Lincoln County Courthouse in Newport, 1958. Voters approved transfer of the county seat from Toledo to Newport in 1952. (Roger A. Hart)

END NOTES
1. "Will Celebrate Highway Opening," *Yaquina Bay News*, 21 Aug. 1924.
2. "Would Move County Seat," *Yaquina Bay News*, 22 March 1928.
3. "Lacking Unity of Efforts," *Newport Journal*, 8 Feb. 1928.
4. "Would Move County Seat."
5. "Wants Highway Routed Through Toledo," *Newport Journal*, 25 Jan. 1928.
6. "Start Movement to Change County Seat," *Newport Journal*, 21 March 1928.
7. "More Propaganda," *Newport Journal*, 28 March 1928.
8. "Yaquina Bay Bridge Hearing," *Yaquina Bay News*, 7 June 1928.
9. "File Notice of Intention to Move County Seat," *Newport Journal*, 27 June 1928.
10. "Newport County Seat Club Rolling," *Lincoln County Leader*, 28 June 1928.
11. Untitled editorial, *Lincoln County Leader*, 5 July 1928.
12. "Newport Passes Bond Issue by Big Majority," *Newport Journal*, 01 Aug. 1928.
13. "Toledo Organizes in County Seat Scrap," *Lincoln County Leader*, 23 Aug. 1928.
14. "County Courthouse May be Moved to Taft," *Beach Resort News*, 10 Aug. 1928.
15. "Another Opportunity," *Newport Journal*, 14 March 1928.
16. "Reducing Rail Service," *Newport Journal*, 29 Aug. 1928.
17. "Another Opportunity."
18. "Courthouse Squabble is Now in High Gear," *Lincoln County Leader*, 23 Oct. 1952.

YAQUINA BAY BRIDGE

AND A NEW NEWPORT

Its steel and concrete arches skip across Yaquina Bay like a perfectly thrown rock, providing a picturesque backdrop for tourists' snapshots. For residents, however, it's far more than an architectural wonder: it's a historic monument to hope, hard work, and the promise of economic prosperity.

Yaquina Bay Bridge was built in the 1930s when the Oregon Coast, like much of the nation, was in the midst of a deep economic depression. When federal money became available through President Roosevelt's Works Progress Administration, the Oregon State Highway Commission applied for more than $5 million for construction of five bridges along the coast. More than $1 million was earmarked for construction of Yaquina Bay Bridge. The federal government, wanting to relieve the economic depression quickly by creating jobs, cautioned the highway commission to produce detailed plans as soon as possible or funds would be directed elsewhere.[1]

Later that same month, janitors at the state capitol building were shocked when they walked into an office full

Opposite: Yaquina Bay Bridge, 1936. Hundreds of Lincoln County men who lost their jobs because of the Great Depression found work building the bridge, a Works Progress Administration project.

Under the supervision of designer Conde B. McCullough, plans for Yaquina Bay and four other coastal bridges were drawn in just three months.

of engineers hard at work at 6 a.m. It was a rare day when the Engineering Department was on the job at that early hour. Double shifts of designers and engineers began planning five Coast Highway bridges under the supervision of Conde B. McCullough.[2] In just three months, they drew plans for the Yaquina Bay Bridge, Alsea Bay Bridge (Waldport), Siuslaw River Bridge (Florence), Umpqua River Bridge (Reedsport), and the Coos Bay Bridge (North Bend).[3] Despite some arguments from lumber interests in favor of wood construction, all plans called for cement and steel.[4]

By January 1934, the coast bridge system plans were not only complete, they had been endorsed by the federal government and the Oregon Legislature. The Yaquina Bay Bridge was to be 38-1/2 feet wide and 6/10ths of a mile long, with a main span of 600 feet.[5] When word of approval reached Newport, an impromptu parade was held and there was general merrymaking among the town's 1,500 inhabitants. A newspaper article announcing approval of the plans added, "Newport and Lincoln County have suffered severely since the depression set in, and the feeling of relief brought great joy."[6]

The long-term effects of the bridge on transportation and the economy were seldom, if ever, discussed in the local paper. The focus was on jobs: the bridge was going to put people back to work.

Although locals were happy with the massive project's approval, they could not have been too surprised. Months before the official go-ahead, lands were acquired at South Beach for a state park. Sam Boardman, state park engineer who led his agency in the creation of 146 parks, told reporters it was desirable for his agency to acquire the park site "in order to eliminate . . . the usual cluttering up of cheap hot dog stands and unsightly cheap eating joints that might otherwise mar the entrance to the most picturesque bridge on the Oregon Coast Highway."[7] A few months later, the parks department also acquired the Yaquina Bay Lighthouse Reservation (located at the north end of the bridge) for the same reasons.[8] Once land was acquired, workers from another federal job-creation program, the Civilian Conservation Corps (CCC), began park construction. The CCC workers for these projects were based out of Otter Rock at what was called "Camp

Newport."[9]

The excitement of the upcoming bridge construction may have dampened when the Highway Commission announced there would be a toll of twenty cents for each auto and five cents for each additional passenger on each of the five bridges. Toll for buses was set at ninety cents, trucks at sixty cents.[10] But for many motorists, this was a small price to pay for the convenience of not having to wait for a ferry ride across the bay. A few months later, a bill passed the legislature designating all five of the coast bridges toll-free.[11]

The toll was not the only controversial issue relating to the Yaquina Bay Bridge; the placement of a new route for Highway 101 through Newport also was the subject of much heated discussion. One faction supported Fifth Street (now Ninth Street) because it was less expensive. The other supported Sixth Street (now Highway 101) because it ran through the central business district. When Sixth Street was widened to accommodate the new highway, several buildings were moved; perhaps most notably was the IOOF (Independent Order of Odd Fellows) Building at the corner of Hurbert and 101. At first there was talk of cutting twenty feet off the front of the turn-of-the-century, three-story building, which at that time housed the post office. This idea was discarded and instead the building was moved back six feet. The newspaper described the move as "no picnic undertaking."[12] The move of this building and the one behind it facing Hurbert Street was successful. The

Tip Top Motors building at the intersection of Alder Street also stood in the way of the new highway. The Highway Commission cut twenty feet from its front and built an addition to the north end to compensate the owners for their loss.

All controversy and relocation aside, August 14, 1934, was a red-letter day for Newport. The first bridge test pile was driven successfully; construction was under way.[13] More than 200 men were employed by the Gilpin and General Construction Companies. The weekly payroll amounted to as much as $5,000 per week. Local merchants also benefited from the roughly $100 each week spent on equipment repairs.[14] Skilled positions went to electricians

Building Yaquina Bay Bridge meant motorists would no longer have to wait for a ferry ride across the bay. Below is the Sadie B. ferry in 1936.

Much of the labor in constructing Yaquina Bay Bridge was done by hand. Workers were placed on a six-day, thirty-hour work week to allow two shifts per day.

and iron workers with bridge or dam building experience. Many local unemployed millworkers were put to work in positions requiring more muscle than skill or experience.

The Consolidated Highway Company employed 160 men to construct hard surface roads leading to the north and south approaches of the bridge. Local restaurants, hotels, and auto camps suddenly shifted into high gear, busier than they had been in years.

According to one man who worked on the project, much of the labor was done by hand. Use of machinery was kept to a minimum to create as many jobs as possible. Workers were placed on a six-day, thirty-hour work week, enabling two shifts a day. When Paul Towsley (1918-1984) got a job on the project, he started at forty-five cents an hour with a penny a day taken out for insurance.[15]

When word got out about the Yaquina Bay con-

struction job, about a dozen unemployed men came to the site each day looking for work. According to Ken Bach, who worked on the bridge crew as a carpenter helper, "If anybody goofed up or slowed down he was fired on the spot and one of these guys got to go to work."[16]

Bridge construction was "no picnic undertaking" on a much larger scale. Swift currents posed an incredible challenge in placing Pier No. 2, which required a 100-hour continuous pour of 2,200 yards of concrete. When a concrete pour began, it continued 24 hours a day no matter how bad the weather. Remembered Towsley, "Sometimes it was so foggy from the cement mixer you couldn't see where you were going to pour."[17] Pier No. 3, located at the south end of the main arch, was the largest and most challenging because of its placement on sand. More than 700

High above Yaquina Bay in driving rain and wind, workers risked their lives to build the bridge. Sadly, there was one fatality. (Oregon Department of Transportation)

193

Above: Finishing touches on the art deco concrete work for which McCullough bridges are known.

Opposite: Closing in on completion of the main arch, March 10, 1936. (Oregon Department of Transportation)

wooden pilings were driven 50 feet below the channel bed of No. 3. Workers on the highest span were 135 feet above the water in high winds and driving rain.[18]

In 1986, Ken Bach recalled that his father, who was foreman over the carpentry crew, discovered an error in the site survey. The placement of the south end of the bridge was a little off to the east. "The original survey work had nailed the south side marker on a board between two pine trees. They shot all lines from that marker. When the wind was from the west, it threw all measurements off to the east." If this had not been discovered, construction on the south end of the bridge would not have aligned with the work in progress on the north end.[19]

Although falls were commonplace, the only fatality on the massive project came three months prior to completion of the bridge when 36-year-old Ted McDaniel fell 110 feet to his death while peeling away wooden framework.[20]

A much happier day was to come as construction wound down. Special arrangements were made to allow Dr. F. M. Carter to be driven across the bridge. Carter, ninety-three, had been an active participant in a great deal of Yaquina Bay's history. In 1863, he was employed as a schoolteacher in Newport. In 1874, he was appointed physician at the Siletz Indian Reservation, where he remained for ten years. He also had practices in Elk City and Newport. In 1895, he opened a drug store in Yaquina City. Dr. Carter, who was said to have resembled Abraham Lincoln in his younger days, did not make a great deal of

money, but as he put it, he "had a lot of friends."[21] When Carter intently gazed at the ocean from the highest point of the bridge, he remarked, "We don't appreciate what we have — Oregon is the finest state in the union, and Newport is the grandest city."[22] Carter, who died a year later, had seen the infamous muddy trails of the area evolve into a magnificent interstate highway system.

A couple of weeks later, on September 6, 1936, the bridge was opened to traffic. In its first 10 hours, a steady stream of 5,190 cars crossed the bridge.[23]

Despite a thick fog, 3,000 people attended the grand opening of the Yaquina Bay Bridge on Oct. 3, 1936. Included in the merrymaking was a parade in which the Ladies Drum & Bugle Corps of Toledo participated.

The Newport Young Men Business Club was put in charge of the official dedication gala to be held October 3, 1936. First up was to be a salute to President Roosevelt, who had been invited to the ceremony but was unable to attend. Designer Conde McCullough also was unable to attend as he was in Costa Rica designing bridges for the Inter-American Highway. Despite the absence of the president and McCullough, and the presence of a thick fog that blinded the entire coast, 3,000 people turned out to listen to speeches by dignitaries from all over the state. This was followed by another round of general merrymaking and a parade which included the Ladies Drum Corps of Toledo. A scheduled flyover by sea planes was canceled because of the fog. Fireworks were shot off but they were shrouded in fog. Later that night, a banquet was held at the Abbey Hotel with Mayor Carson of Portland as toastmaster.[24]

Perhaps the only note of sadness came when the end of the ferries was fully realized.[25] The ferries' crews, their bellowing horns, and motorists killing time on the Bayfront while waiting for a ride across the bay were all sights and sounds now part of an era gone by.

The dedication ceremonies were complete but the bridge was not; detail work remained. All five of the McCullough bridges built at this time included subtle art deco embellishments. Ken Bach pointed out that all this detail work was done with wood; concrete simply filled in the shapes that he and the other carpenters nailed together.[26] A few weeks after the dedication ceremony, the local newspaper matter-of-factly announced in its November 19, 1936, edition, "Yaquina Bay Bridge is completed and the workmen were discharged Tuesday. Two years, three months and seventeen days have elapsed since construction began." In the course of construction, 25,000 cubic yards of earth were moved, 30,000 cubic yards of concrete

To build the Yaquina Bay Bridge, 25,000 cubic yards of earth were moved, 30,000 cubic yards of concrete poured and more than 3,000 tons of steel bolted and welded into place. This aerial view was taken in September 1947. (Roger A. Hart)

197

poured and more than 3,000 tons of steel bolted and welded into place.

After completion of the bridge and the S-shape stretch of Highway 101 through Newport, a reshaping of the town began as merchants relocated to buildings facing Highway 101. In the early 1930s, the east side of the highway between Angle and Hurbert streets was lined with about five houses. One of the most substantial businesses to move to this block was the Bank of Newport. A Bayfront institution since 1925, the bank moved into a new $17,000 building constructed at 101 and Angle in 1937; it featured private customer booths and a vault with eighteen-inch-thick walls.[27] That same year, William McKevitt opened the Midway Theater next-door.[28] About the time the theater opened, the Miller Brothers, who had operated a jewelry store in Toledo since 1924, opened a branch store in McKevitt's new building. Charles Miller told a reporter,

"We are opening a branch in Newport because we believe that the coast section of the county is going to prosper and we intend to grow with the community."[29] Also in 1937, Charles Boddy opened a

The Yaquina Bay Bridge and the completion of Highway 101 reshaped Newport. Businesses moved from Nye Beach and the Bayfront to take advantage of the visibility 101 had to offer. This photo was taken March 24, 1960. (Roger A. Hart)

bowling alley just up from 101 on Hurbert in the bottom floor of the skating rink.[30] A.L. Thomas, who owned an agate shop in Nye Beach since 1895, opened a store on Highway 101.[31] These are just a few of the many who made the move to the downtown business district. Later in the 1950s, growth headed north along the highway.

This photo was taken Sept. 12, 1948.
(Roger A. Hart)

Ever since the earliest discussions and planning of Yaquina Bay Bridge construction, jobs for unemployed workers were usually mentioned in the same breath. The real purpose of the bridge was to give the economy of the coast a shot in the arm, which it certainly did. Perhaps to the surprise of many, the bridge had a much more dramatic effect on Newport. Tourism shot up seventy-two percent. Two major business districts, the Bayfront and Nye Beach, were bypassed by Highway 101, forcing the development of a third district (called city center) along the highway. For decades after completion of construction, Newport grew mainly along Highway 101. Ever since traffic crossed the bridge for the first time, Newport has been represented by the very thing that redefined it, the Yaquina Bay Bridge.

END NOTES
1. "Oregon to Share $3,000,000,000 Fund," *Yaquina Bay News*, 22 June 1933.
2. "Two Shifts Work on Bridge Plans," *Yaquina Bay News*, 22 June 1933.
3. "Coast Bridge Plans Completed," *Yaquina Bay News*, 14 Sept. 1933.
4. "Wooden Bridges," *Yaquina Bay News*, 06 July 1933.
5. "Yaquina Bridge Gets Approved," *Yaquina Bay News*, 12 Oct. 1933.
6. "Coast Highway Bridges Approved," *Yaquina Bay News*, 11 Jan. 1934.
7. "South Beach Park Desired by State," *Yaquina Bay News*, 02 Nov. 1933.
8. "Newport Will Have State Park," *Yaquina Bay News*, 05 April 1934.
9. "Locate 5 CCC Camps on the Coast," *Yaquina Bay News*, 20 Sept. 1934.
10. "Toll on Coast Bridges are Set," *Yaquina Bay News*, 05 July 1934.
11. "5 Coast Bridges to be Toll-Free," *Yaquina Bay News*, 14 Feb. 1934.
12. "Contractors Start Tuesday To Move I.O.O.F. Hall," *Yaquina Bay News*, 19 July 1934.
13. "First Test Pile Driven in Construction of Bridge," *Yaquina Bay News*, 16 Aug. 1934.
14. Joseph Patterson, "Yaquina Bay Bridge Will be Inspiration to Travelers," *Yaquina Bay News*, 25 April 1935.
15. Paul Towsley, interviewer unknown, 11

A bridgeworker rides his bicycle across a beam on a five-dollar bet, ca. 1936.

July 1978, transcription, OCHC archives, Newport.

16. Mike Thoele, "Yaquina Bridge Spans Bay, 50 years," *Register-Guard*, 27 Sept. 1986.

17. Towsley.

18. "Coast Highway Completed by Opening of Yaquina Bay Bridge on Sunday," *Newport Journal*, 09 Sept. 1936.

19. Thoele.

20. "Ted McDaniel Falls From Bridge," *Newport Journal*, 22 July 1936.

21. "Dr. Carter, Newport Patriarch, Looks Back on Eventful Life," *Yaquina Bay News*, 06 June 1935.

22. "Dr. F.M. Carter, Aged 94, Crosses Yaquina Bay Bridge," *Yaquina Bay News*, 22 August 1936.

23. Untitled, *Yaquina Bay News*, 08 October 1936.

24. "Bridge Dedication Held Saturday," *Newport Journal*, 07 Oct. 1936.

25. "Yaquina Bridge Proves Popular," *Yaquina Bay News*, 10 Sept. 1936.

26. Thoele.

27. "New Bank Officially Opened," *Newport Journal*, 03 Nov. 1937.

28. "NW Theater Opened Friday," *Newport Journal*, 24 Nov. 1937.

29. "Will Open New Jewelry Store," *Newport Journal*, 10 Nov. 1937.

30. "Bowling Alley to Open," *Newport Journal*, 12 May 1937.

31. "Erecting New Store Building," *Newport Journal*, 06 Jan. 1937.

The graceful arches of Yaquina Bay Bridge have become a favorite backdrop for photographers. Here Roger A. Hart used them to frame Miss Newport of 1947, Helen McFetridge.

Roger A. Hart

Chronicler of the Coast

"Hart's for Parts." Longtime Newport residents probably remember this slogan of the local Napa Auto Parts dealership owned and operated by Roger Hart. Another of his slogans could have been "Hart's for History": Hart was an avid photographer for most of his life, and the fruit of his labors provides a lasting photographic record of Lincoln County.

Hart has donated to the Lincoln County Historical Society several hundred photographs, negatives, 16 mm films, and slides chronicling this region from the 1930s into the 1980s. Reprints of his images are a staple of *The Bayfront* magazine and have appeared in countless other publications, videos, and exhibits. His images also have aided land-use and environmental researchers and historic preservationists. They have proven to be an invaluable addition to the collective memory of Lincoln County.

Hart's photographs are historically significant for several reasons. They are of exceptional quality, taken by a talented photographer whose eye for composition becomes evident even in his earliest images. They are well docu-

Opposite: Roger Hart especially enjoyed photographing the picturesque fishing boats at Newport's Bayfront. This picture was taken on Sept. 11, 1949.

Hart ran a successful auto parts store on Highway 101 for nearly thirty years before retiring in 1966.

mented: without fail, Hart recorded the date and subject of every photo. And they capture on film a subject overlooked by most photographers but important to historians: everyday things. Hart's passion for taking photos resulted in some of the county's most significant records of buildings, street scenes, working life, recreation, political events, and local personalities.

This author interviewed Roger Hart in April 1995. Hart recalled he acquired his first camera, a folding, roll-film Kodak, during his freshman year in high school in Newberg. He tried out his new toy at the football field, where the Newberg team was practicing. He took several shots of the players and developed the prints in a small darkroom he had set up at home. When Hart showed the prints to his classmates, they immediately asked to purchase reprints. He used the proceeds to purchase more photo supplies. Perhaps it was this positive reinforcement that sparked an interest in photography that never diminished. At the time of the interview, Hart was eighty-nine years old and still keeping a top-of-the-line 35 mm camera on hand just in case a photo opportunity should arise.

Hart's attention to detail developed before he started taking photos. His father, a blacksmith and farmer, made the transition to the automobile age and became an auto mechanic and dealer of Willys-Overland and Chrysler cars. His son, who did not care for selling or fixing cars, went to work as clerk in the auto parts department. After he finished school, he was given half interest in his dad's operation. Keeping track of inventory and accounts

Because Hart always kept a camera at the ready, he was able to capture these boys playing on top of a sinking car on Nye Beach on Sept. 22, 1945.

Above: Hart took this photo in Newport in April 1946.

Opposite: Hart chronicled scenes in Newport and Lincoln County from the 1930s into the 1980s. The top photo is looking west on Front Street (Newport's Bayfront) at Fall Street on Oct. 7, 1945. The bottom photo is the same view on March 24, 1979.

payable and receivable taught Hart to value organization and attention to detail. His skill at managing inventory transferred well to managing his ever-growing photo collection.

During the depression of the 1930s, the family business fell on hard times. Newberg had too many auto dealerships for its depressed economy. Hart sensed that things might be better elsewhere. In 1936, when the last link of the Oregon Coast Highway was completed with the Yaquina Bay Bridge, Hart believed the coast would prosper with the increased auto traffic. He and his wife, Dorthea, traveled the new highway from Oceanlake (now Lincoln City) to Yachats, stopping at gas stations and garages to inquire about the availability of car parts. They concluded Newport would be a good central location to start an auto parts store.

In February 1937, Hart found a small storefront in the Wills Building next to Carrick's grocery store on Highway 101 that rented for twenty-five dollars a month. Hart was off to a very modest start. When the Napa Auto Parts executives discovered Hart had opened a parts store in Newport and had paid the bills from the Newberg store despite its difficulties, they set him up with a complete inventory of parts on consignment. Hart's assumption

Hart was actively involved in the Chamber of Commerce and was the official photographer for the Crab Festival. Below is the 1947 Miss Newport delegation at the Crab Festival. Front and center is Miss Newport, Helen McFetridge; Marvin Uhlenhake sits to the left of her and Newport Mayor Martin Skriver to her right. In the back row are Margaret Bookhamer, Florene Jackson, and Jean Gardner.

about the economy on the coast was correct. His business quickly outgrew its space, so Hart moved across Highway 101 to the Anderson Building. Later Hart constructed his own building on the northwest corner of Lee and Highway 101. Hart's arrangement with the Napa organization lasted until his retirement and sale of the business in 1966.

Prior to Hart's relocation to Newport, the town had no auto parts store or professional photographers (A.L. Thomas, Newport's best-known photographer, was in failing health and died not long after Hart came to town). With Hart's arrival, the town had both. When word got out about his photographic skills, Hart was asked to take pictures of weddings and family reunions and to make reprints of photos for locals. After his business was established, Hart had the luxury of taking a day off now and then. This free time was spent doing his favorite activity: taking pictures, especially of fishing boats on the Bayfront. Hart, who seldom used a tripod, used light and reflection beautifully to capture the personalities of Newport's varied fishing fleet.

Hart assumed an active role in the community and, of course, produced a photographic chronicle in the process. He was heavily involved in the Chamber of Commerce and the Crab Festival, an annual event that brought thousands of people to Newport for a free crab lunch and festivities. Hart was chosen to accompany Andy

Hart photo of Myer's Moorage in Newport, Aug. 29, 1954.

209

Naterlin, Jim Howes, and other prominent Lincoln County businessmen who promoted the festival by traveling all over the state, "talking to whoever would listen" and giving them free crabs. Hart also did work at his own cost for the Lincoln County Historical Society, the school district, and the Miss Newport contest.

As a result of his active role in the community, his attention to detail, and his love of photography, Hart created a priceless historic record of Newport and Lincoln County for future generations.

Mrs. Frances Ziemieczuk, Newport's first and only female motorcycle officer, July 23, 1948.

Above: Junction Garage in Waldport, June 1943.
Left: Pixie Kitchen in Lincoln City, 1959.

*Right: Crab
Festival feed on
the Bayfront,
May 1949.*

*Opposite page:
Queen of the
first Crab
Festival in
1938 was
Maxine Omlid,
center.*

CRUSTACEANS AND THE COLD WAR

Imagine a town of about 2,000 visited by 25,000 people in one day. This was the case in Newport in 1938. Why would 25,000 people flock to Newport? A free lunch.

May Day 1938 was the first of Newport's annual Crab Festivals, and to celebrate the town treated its guests to 6,000 crabs. Bay Boulevard (then called Front Street) was closed to one lane of traffic. Tables ran end to end for the full length of the business district. Crabs were handed to motorists as they drove past what must have been Newport's first drive-through window (only without the window). Maxine Omlid was crowned queen of the Crab Festival. After the banquet, the street department employed a dump truck and two men for three days to sweep up the cracked crab shells.

There were two reasons for bringing the crowds and the mess into town. The price of dungeness crab had hit rock bottom because no one was eating crab, and organizers thought the festival would create a craving for the crustacean that would last long after the festival was over. Secondly, tourism on the central Oregon Coast needed a shot in the arm. With the completion of the Yaquina Bay Bridge, the Bayfront had been bypassed. Motorists traveling the coast highway no longer had to drive to the Bayfront to catch the ferry across Yaquina Bay. The Great Depression also added to Newport's economic woes.

The idea for the Crab Festival came from Andrew Naterlin, a town promoter who later served as mayor of Newport (1940-1947) and in the Oregon Legislature (1957-1969). His fellow legislators nicknamed him "Senator 101" for his undying lobbying efforts for funds to improve the coastal highway. Naterlin also was known for being the only blind legislator in the United States. But he did not set out to be a politician. Naterlin owned his first commercial fishing boat at age nineteen. He came to Newport from Astoria in 1928 and later managed the New England Fish Company in Newport. He learned the legislative ropes when he lobbied as manager of the Yaquina plant of Newport Fish Co. Naterlin, who died in 1985, was honored in 1977 when Newport named a community center after him. Naterlin dreamed up the Crab Festival and served for many years as its organizer.[1]

Naterlin thought that given the promise of a free

crab meal, people would flock to the Bayfront and develop an enduring taste for crab. Without a doubt, Naterlin was onto something. The second year of the festival, 30,000 people came to Newport for their free meal. They also were treated to live music, a Siletz tribal dance, boat races, and, of course, the crowning of the festival queen. In 1941, Newport fishermen harvested 15,000 crabs for the festival despite bad weather. The biggest crab caught was awarded to the person traveling the farthest to the festival.[2]

Unusual and oftentimes elaborate schemes were cooked up to generate interest. For the 1939 festival, special hats were made from the backs of jumbo crabs and worn by Newporters to publicize the event. Naterlin and a delegation of festival promoters traveled around the state giving out crab. The state capitol building and the offices of the *Oregonian* and other newspapers were some of their well-

Opposite page: Andrew Naterlin founded the Crab Festival to boost tourism and generate an enduring taste for crab. (Roger A. Hart)

Above: Crab Festival promoters traveled around the state handing out crabs as publicity stunts. In this 1948 photo, Dudley Turncliff, at left, presents a crab to Oregonian Editor Ben Hur Lampman. On the right are Harry Hale, Oregonian production manager, and Naterlin. (Roger A. Hart)

215

publicized stops.

When World War II broke out, Newport became concerned with blackouts, the possibility of an enemy invasion on the coast, and winning the war. Some fishermen went off to fight; others turned their boats over to the military for patrolling the coast; still others fished for soupfin shark, the livers of which were fed to soldiers to improve their night vision. The Crab Festival fell by the wayside.[3]

After the war, the festival came back in a big way. It outgrew the Bayfront, so events were held throughout Newport. For the Crab Festival of 1947, the Natatorium ballroom at Nye Beach (now the site of the turnaround parking lot) was the scene of the coronation of Toledo's Joan Balderee as the Crab Festival Queen. Mayor Martin Skriver presented Queen Joan with a crown made of gold and polished agates. It was designed and handcrafted by A. L. Thomas, who had a curio and lapidary shop at Nye Beach. In 1950, a new crown was made with a gold framework decorated with small crabs covered with glittering sequins. If the coronation of the queen and a free crab meal were not enough to entice tourists to the 1947 festival, how about the chance to win a new car? Organizers raffled off a brand new Hudson sedan, donated by Williams Motor Co. of

Above: In the late 1940s the Crab Festival had outgrown the Bayfront. This parade is headed south on Highway 101. (Roger A. Hart)

Newport.

Eventually the festival fell on hard times. Crabs became too expensive to give away and the festival lost money. In 1951, the last Crab Festival was held. By this time promoters had elevated its status to the "National Crab Festival." The festival went out with a bang: thirty-eight cases of crabs were loaded onto a C-47 transport plane, flown to Oakland, California, and transhipped to soldiers stationed in Korea. [4]

In 1953, the May celebration was replaced with Loyalty Days. Lincoln County veterans organizations held a modest parade "in support of a counter demonstration of the annual May Day mass rallies and celebrations staged by the communists." This Cold War-era display of patriotism originated with the national Veterans of Foreign Wars, which began celebrating Loyalty Days in the late 1940s. In 1958, President Eisenhower signed a Loyalty Days Proclamation. It was thought this holiday was "a most effective counter to the disorderly demonstrations of Communist May Day." [5]

Loyalty Days grew in popularity. By 1970, parade entries totaled nearly 100. The 1970 Loyalty Days Festival still contained many elements from the Crab Festival, including a dungeness crab dinner offered for $1.75 in the parking lot of the Abbey on the Bayfront. Demonstrations

Prize drawings drew a big crowd to Newport's City Center at the 1949 festival.
(Gilmour)

Cars and pedestrians vie for space on Highway 101 at the 1947 festival.
(Roger A. Hart)

of crab pot construction and net making and repair were held, not to mention shrimp picking and fish filleting contests. Air shows, boat races, horse shows, scuba diving contests, and crab running contests have all been Loyalty Days events. In 1968, Gov. Tom McCall and officials from the Army Corps of Engineers were on hand to cut a ribbon which ran across Yaquina Bay to mark completion of the harbor improvements made in the previous eighteen years.

Over the years, the focus of Newport's two festivals changed from creating a market for crab and drawing tourists to a display of patriotism. Though the passage of the Cold War has diminished the need for a patriotic May Day festival, Loyalty Days has outlasted the Cold War to evolve into Newport's celebration of community pride and the beginning of spring.

END NOTES
1. Scrapbook complied by Dorothy Naterlin, Oregon Coast History Center, #84.88.1.
2. "Crab Festival Attracts Thousands," *Newport Journal*, 10 May 1939.
3. Scrapbook.
4. Hugh Scott, "Loading of Crabmeat for Korea Launches Newport's Fete," *The Oregonian*, 20 May 1951.
5. Newport Chamber of Commerce press release, 1967, "Loyalty Day Background," original in papers compiled by Stan Allyn, Oregon Coast History Center, #93.16.1.

Opposite: The 1949 Festival Court took a ride in a crab box for its photo opportunity.
(Gilmour)

THE FIGHTING, FISHING KINGFISHER

When Stan Allyn (1913-1992) dreamed of the ultimate charter boat, he wasted no time finding a piece of paper and sketching the design as best he could. Although he had no experience in boat design, Allyn took his plan to the builders at Westerlund Boat and Machine Works in Portland and put them to work on his vision. Allyn's plan called for a distinctive, oceangoing charter boat with an aerodynamic bow, spacious railed foredeck, and a pulpit extending over the open water beyond the bow.[1] In June 1941, the *Kingfisher* was launched. Now on the National Historic Register, the *Kingfisher* is well-known to residents and visitors alike as the flagship of the Depoe Bay Tradewinds Charters fleet.[2]

Allyn hastily drew the plan for the *Kingfisher* on a piece of butcher paper in

Left: Stan Allyn, ca. 1940. Though Allyn had no experience in design, he drew plans for a boat that was to become a model for all charter boats, the Kingfisher.

Opposite: The Kingfisher dressed up for the Fleet of Flowers in Depoe Bay, May 30, 1971. (Stan Allyn)

September 1940 while living at the Trollers Lodge, a Depoe Bay motel. A copy of this plan still hangs in Room No. 3, the very room in which it was drawn.[3] The original plan now resides in the Oregon Coast History Center's archives.

When the fifty-foot-long *Kingfisher* docked in Depoe Bay for the first time, it was by far the biggest and best charter boat in the harbor. Much to Allyn's surprise, though, the *Kingfisher* was used as a charter boat for only four months. "War clouds were brewing and the armed forces needed a good source of vitamin A and B for night patrols," Allyn recalled later.[4] That source was soupfin shark, whose liver brought an incredible $20 a pound. Allyn outfitted his prized boat with commercial trolling gear and struck out to make his fortune. After the waters from Depoe Bay to Cascade Head were fished out, Allyn headed south to a new base of operations, Coos Bay, where he arrived Thanksgiving Day 1941.

On December 7, Allyn, on board the *Kingfisher*, heard the news that Pearl Harbor had been attacked. Allyn rushed over to the Coos Bay Coast Guard Station to join the

Stan Allyn with his first boat, a Columbia River gillnetter with which he started his charter boat business.

"FIGHTING KINGFISHER"

war effort and offer the use of his prized $10,000 boat to the Coast Guard. Allyn was made a Boatswain's Mate First Class, and he and the *Kingfisher* patrolled the waters between Coos Bay and Astoria.

Later Allyn and the *Kingfisher* parted company when he was accepted in the Coast Guard Academy. Allyn then saw service as a skipper of a sub chaser in the Atlantic and in the Okinawa invasion in the South Pacific. Meanwhile, the *Kingfisher* patrolled the coast for the duration of the war.[5]

The *Kingfisher* and Allyn were reunited when the two were released from duty at war's end. The *Kingfisher* was rerigged for charter fishing after it returned to Depoe Bay in spring 1946. Everything was as it had been — except the *Kingfisher*'s beautiful wood finish. The boat's white-cedar hull had been painted in camouflage when it entered the war effort. The military paint had been absorbed into the wood, making it impossible to sand away. So Allyn painted it white with blue and red trim, which it remains to

When Allyn heard about the bombing of Pearl Harbor, he offered his beloved Kingfisher *to the Coast Guard for patrolling along the Oregon Coast. Though they were separated during the war, skipper and boat were reunited at war's end.*

this day.[6]

Shortly after the war, the *Kingfisher* was equipped with a typewriter. Allyn took a writing course under the GI bill and became a correspondent for the *Oregonian* and other newspapers.

WAR IS OVER - HOME IN DEPOE BAY !

The *Kingfisher* was his favorite place to write.[7]

In 1947, Allyn had two smaller, thirty-seven-foot versions of the *Kingfisher* built at Ed Gerttula's Siletz Boat Yard at Kernville: the *Tradewinds Sportfisher* and the *Tradewinds Fleetfisher*.[8] Soon the *Kingfisher* became the model for Northwest boat builders. Many of the charter boats that appeared in the post-war era in Depoe Bay and

Top: Immediately after the war, Allyn (with life ring) rerigged the Kingfisher *for charter fishing and painted the camouflaged hull white with blue and red trim, which it remains to this day.*

Bottom: Two women identified as "Dana" and "Mattoviah" on the Kingfisher *pulpit, ca. 1950.*

226

other Northwest ports were smaller versions of the *Kingfisher*. When the Coast Guard began its inspection program for charter boats in 1958, the *Kingfisher* saw service once again: this time as the model for establishing requirements for all vessels carrying passengers for hire in the region.[9]

Since the advent of fiberglass, wooden-hull charter boats such as the *Kingfisher* have become increasingly scarce. Despite tightening regulations that are more difficult to meet for wooden-hull boats, the *Kingfisher* continues to pass its annual inspection (as of this writing) and take hoards of thrill-seekers out onto the ocean for sightseeing and whale watching. Each summer as many as 30,000 people take excursions aboard the *Kingfisher*, the oldest charter vessel still in operation in Oregon.

Perhaps no one can remember his first excursion aboard the *Kingfisher* more vividly than Dan Zimmerman. His first encounter with the *Kingfisher* was in 1960 as a child, hanging onto the railing of the pulpit. Even with the active imagination of a youngster, Zimmerman probably did not envision himself as skipper of the *Kingfisher*. Twenty-nine years later, Stan Allyn honored Zimmerman by entrusting the *Kingfisher* to him.[10]

Zimmerman, who served as skipper of the *Kingfisher* for eighteen years, spent many of his days off refinishing the wood trim and removing alterations to restore and maintain the *Kingfisher*'s original appearance as much as possible. Zimmerman returned the honor to Allyn

Top: *A woman sits in the crow's nest on the* Kingfisher, *ca. 1950.*

in 1991 when he secured the *Kingfisher*'s spot in history by placing it on the National Register of Historic Places.

Whether or not in service, Stan Allyn's *Kingfisher* will remain the flagship of Depoe Bay.

STAN THE MAN

In 1936, with no money left to continue his education, Stan Allyn left Oregon Agricultural College (now Oregon State University) to start a new life as newspaper circulation manager for the *Portland News-Telegram*. After securing employment, Allyn purchased a converted Columbia River gillnetting boat for $350 "just for kicks" and began refurbishing it. He spent his spare time aboard his boat he christened *Tradewinds* learning to navigate on the Willamette and Columbia rivers. In 1938, he again wanted to start a new life. Allyn headed downriver to the ocean with his sights set on "The World's Smallest Natural Harbor," Depoe Bay.[11] By his own admission, Allyn knew almost nothing about ocean fishing or operating an oceangoing boat, yet he wanted to do both.

Lacking faith in the old gill-netter's engine, Allyn equipped the boat with backup power — a pair of sails — before venturing into the ocean. Allyn's first attempt to sail to Depoe Bay was thwarted when his boat took a beating as he attempted to cross the Columbia River bar in conditions far too rough for the frail gill-netter. (The Coast Guard headed him off, probably saving him from imminent disaster.) Later in the journey, the engine conked out at least twice. Despite the rocky start, Allyn forged ahead.[12]

A group of nuns are blessed with a hefty catch during one of the Kingfisher's charter trips, ca. 1965. (Stan Allyn)

Depoe Bay fishermen, concerned for Allyn and his potential passengers' safety, showed him the ropes. Allyn was informed that charter boats trolled with deep water "meat lines" that had at least twenty pounds of lead and six baited leaders attached.[13] The paying passengers watched the crew fish and at the end of the excursion divided the catch equally. Allyn felt sport fishing should be more fun. "So I went up to Portland and bought six of the cheapest rods and reels I could find, because it was all I could afford, and snuck them aboard my boat so the others wouldn't get mad at me for trying something different. It gave passengers a semblance of sportfishing."[14]

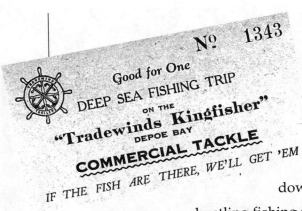

N⁰ 1343

Good for One
DEEP SEA FISHING TRIP
ON THE
"Tradewinds Kingfisher"
DEPOE BAY
COMMERCIAL TACKLE

IF THE FISH ARE THERE, WE'LL GET 'EM

*Ticket for one deep sea
fishing trip aboard the*
Kingfisher.

Charter fishing, which required a steady stream of thrill-seeking sport fishermen and tourists, was a relatively new and speculative venture; it was an industry in its infancy. Allyn, Depoe Bay's newest charter boat captain, doubled as salesman, pacing up and down the sidewalk of the Depoe Bay Bridge hustling fishing trips aboard the *Tradewinds* for two dollars a head. In the winter, Allyn would return to Portland and take a job in a sawmill or whatever he could get. His efforts paid off. The next year he was able to purchase a second boat. Scarcely a year later, Allyn added another boat to his fleet and not long after that the Tradewinds flagship, the *Kingfisher*, was built.[15]

Allyn also was a vocal advocate of improvements to Depoe Bay. Before the harbor was drained and dredged in 1950, boats were often left stranded high and dry at low tide. The widening of the channel and the installation of a wave break at the entrance of the harbor were other causes Allyn championed. Allyn was honored for his lifetime achievements when both Oregon's governor and the mayor of Depoe Bay officially proclaimed September 22, 1987, as Stan Allyn Day. A plaque commemorating his many contributions to the coastal community was installed at Depoe Bay State Park overlooking the harbor entrance.[16]

After retiring, Allyn devoted much of his time to writing about the sea. He wrote three books: *Heave To!*

You'll Drown Yourselves!, Top Deck 20! Best Coast Sea Stories!,
and *The Day the Sun Didn't Rise — Plus Eight More Sea
Stories and One Un-Sea Story.* Containing Allyn's own experiences at sea and other interesting stories, the books are as
colorful as the man who wrote them.

Allyn did more than start a new life in Depoe Bay.
He championed an industry and a town, and in the
process, became a local legend.

END NOTES
1. "Tradewinds Kingfisher Celebrates 40th Birthday," *The News
Guard*, 25 June 1981.
2. Daniel C. Zimmerman, National Register of Historic Places
Registration Form, 2 Dec. 1990.
3. Loretta Hoagland, owner of Trollers Lodge, interview with
author, 15 April 1994.
4. "Tradewinds Kingfisher Celebrates."
5. Ibid.
6. Zimmerman, section 8, page 1b.
7. "Salt Water Story Writer,"*Oregonian*'s
Northwest Magazine, 31 Oct. 1954.
8. Larry Barber, "Boatbuilders Old Timers
and Not So Old," *Freshwater News,* June 1985.
9. Zimmerman, section 8, page 2.
10. Zimmerman, interview with author, May
1994.
11. Winifred Layton, untitled, *Capital Journal,*
5 Sept. 1970.
12. Stan Allyn, "Broached," *Heave To! You'll
Drown Yourselves!* (Portland: Binford and
Mort), 2-14.
13. Allyn, "Wild Boar's Nest," *Heave To!,* 26-
30.
14. Adelle Altizer, "Captain Stan Shares His
Memories In Book," *News-Times,* 24 Nov.
1982.
15. Ibid.
16. "Stan Allyn Gets His Own Day," *News
Guard*, 31 Sept. 1987.

The Kingfisher *in
Depoe Bay Harbor,
June 1969.
(Stan Allyn)*

TO CATCH A SHARK

FISHING IN THE FORTIES

Scrap metal, flax (linen fiber), and the liver of the soupfin shark: what do these have in common? All three were perceived as vital to United States troops fighting in World War II.

To prevent a shortage of raw material for war machinery, nationwide scrap-metal drives sent the population scrambling for usable metal. Closer to home, Willamette Valley farmers planted flax for the production of parachute lines and fire hoses.

Even closer to home, along the Oregon Coast, the perceived wartime need for oil extracted from soupfin shark livers led to a boom in what was then an industry in its infancy. Just before the United States entered the war, scientists discovered soupfin shark livers were rich in vitamin A, an aid to better night vision -- something American soldiers could use in their battles overseas.

Catching an occasional shark was nothing new for some fishermen; the vitamin A discovery, combined with wartime demand, gave them a major financial incentive to fish for shark. Shark liver oil proved useful to the fisher-

Opposite: Fishing boats on Newport's Bayfront, Oct. 7, 1945. The demand for soupfin shark during World War II provided a much-needed boon to the fishing industry on the Oregon Coast. (Roger A. Hart)

233

men in other ways: back in the days when many commercial fishing boats relied on steam engines for power, oiling the engine's many moving parts was a major expense. To cut costs, thrifty fishermen would catch shark and fry the liver on the engines' hot boiler. The result was an oil suitable for use as a lubricant. When longtime fisherman Norman Chopard was interviewed by a reporter in the 1940s, he recalled one of the boat engineers he worked with used shark liver oil. "You could smell him and his machinery a mile off," Chopard said.

About 1940, Chopard read in a trade publication of a fisherman making good money off soupfin shark in California. Chopard remembered that in years past, he inadvertently had caught some shark that may have been

Drag boat load of dogfish, 1940s. When soupfin shark became depleted, local fishermen switched to this smaller shark variety.

soupfins off the coast of Depoe Bay and Newport. He then put together a crew and began experimenting with different types of gear suitable for catching soupfin shark, which range in size from five to seven feet.[1]

He found the most effective method of catching soupfin shark was to rig very heavy mile-long lines with about 500 evenly spaced hooks baited with "red side" salmon or frozen herring.[2] The end of the line was sunk to the bottom with a heavy boat anchor. After two to three hours, the line would be winched on board with ". . . all manner of bottom fish plus a number of soupfin sharks."[3] A strange requirement for soupfin fishing was a heavy strip of sheet metal from the boat rollers to below the water line. The skin of the soupfin shark was abrasive enough to sand the paint off the boat.[4]

Waters richest in soupfin shark were off California, but the Oregon Coast had a goodly share. Chopard and his partner, Auggie Hammer, shared their discoveries with Newport fisherman Captain T. Solberg of the halibut fishing boat *Holmes*. Solberg re-rigged the *Holmes* for soupfin shark to become the top money-making boat out of Newport that year.[5] In the latter part of 1940, there were twelve boats out of Newport bringing loads of soupfin shark to the Yaquina Bay Fish and New England Fish plants, where the livers were prepared for final processing in Portland or California. Local fish plants were paying from $500 to $700 for a day's shark catch. An added benefit for fishermen was that soupfin season was in the winter,

When this wartime identification card was issued in 1942, Julia Strand was helping her husband on his gillnet boat. At that time, they were selling fish to Yaquina Bay Fish Co.

between salmon, tuna, and halibut seasons.

Local mink farmers also benefited, at least for awhile. They were forced to discontinue feeding their animals leftover shark meat, however, when it was discovered that it caused their fur to turn red.[6] The Newport Lions Club also enjoyed soupfin shark meat at a banquet held at the Abbey Hotel.[7] (No word was given whether their skin turned red.)

Eventually, news about the fantastic money to be made shark fishing worked its way East. Wanna-be fishermen from landlocked states started arriving on the Oregon Coast expecting to get rich. Most were quickly discouraged when they discovered fishing commercially for shark required an ocean-going boat and several thousand dollars worth of equipment.[8] Rough seas also posed a challenge for potential shark fishermen; the catch tended to be better during stormy weather.[9]

As the war grew closer, activity for the entire Yaquina Bay fishing industry picked up considerably. All of the major Yaquina Bay fish plants — Waldport Sea Foods Co., Yaquina Bay Fish Co., Columbia Rivers Packers Association, and New England Fish Co. — underwent large expansions.[10] Soupfin shark, crab, and tuna were the big moneymakers of the day. By July 1941, there were 125 commercial fishing boats running out of Newport. It was estimated that 375 men and women were employed in the fishing fleet and processing plants.[11]

When the United States finally entered World War II in December 1941, the lives and livelihoods of all Americans changed dramatically; those in this area's fishing industry were no exception. A few of the faster boats were lent out to the Coast Guard to patrol the Oregon Coast for a possible enemy invasion. One such boat was Stan Allyn's charter vessel, *Tradewinds Kingfisher*.[12] The *Anna H*, a fast cabin cruiser and charter boat out of Newport, was also turned over by its owners for Coast Guard use.[13]

Locally, a substantial percentage of those employed in the fishing industry went off to war. Others who remained on the coast did their part by catching soupfin shark. Shark liver oil was not the only wartime fishery

Newport's fishing fleet, ca. 1940.

Newport's fishing fleet, taken from a 1940s postcard.

demand; there was a general shortage of all types of meat. Halibut and tuna caught off the Oregon Coast and canned locally helped alleviate the situation. The armed forces purchased as much as three million pounds of fish in a month, at times procuring more fish than meat.[14] Processors and canners found themselves shorthanded. In an article at the top of the front page, the *Newport Journal* pleaded for laborers willing to work for seventy-five cents an hour. "It may be true that there are lots of women and girls here who do not need work, but they should consider the national need for preserving fish for food purposes." The appeal also mentioned that a special nursery school was available for children while their mothers worked. "A telephone call to any of the fish plants is all that is necessary to get a job."[15] By 1944, the Yaquina Bay Fish Co., one of the largest processors at the time, had an average of one hundred employees with a weekly payroll of $5,500.[16]

The fishermen also were making good money; both the demand and price of soupfin shark liver skyrocketed during the war. In 1941, a single shark netted its catcher $100.[17] In December 1942, the Hall brothers of Newport docked in the bay with 500 shark livers caught on their boat, *Mary Francis*. Their catch, made on one setting of their gear, brought them an incredible $9,600. By contrast, the highest tuna catch of 1942 was by Charles Ell of the *Amak*; Ell caught five tons of tuna in a week. The New England Fish Co. wrote him out a check for $1,996 for his cargo.[18]

The glory days of shark fishing were not to last. As the war progressed, soupfins became scarce in both Oregon and California waters. Local fishermen switched over to using drag boats (equipped with a large net) to catch dogfish. Like soupfin, the dogfish, or grayfish, is a type of shark whose liver is rich in vitamin A. By the time the war was over, the shark liver boom had gone bust.

After successfully meeting wartime demands, the fishermen of the central Oregon Coast returned to a peacetime pace of life. In the postwar years, the health of the fishing industry hinged primarily on salmon and tuna catches. Charter fishing also came into its own: the public, tired of the severity of war, wanted to have fun.[19]

It was a get-it-done attitude that enabled local fishermen to meet the demands of World War II. These demands long have been replaced by far more complex resource management issues which continue to challenge fishermen today. The get-it-done attitude will help the fishing fleet of the central Oregon Coast survive while others may not.

NEWPORT'S JAWS

Twenty-eight years before the development of the shark fishing industry on Yaquina Bay, the capture of a single great white shark over sixteen feet long caught the attention of local residents.

In October 1913, while fishing about five miles off Yaquina Head, Captain Cramer of the excursion/commercial fishing vessel *Ollie S* spotted a whale carcass in the water. Cramer and crew wanted to tow it into Yaquina Bay as a tourist attraction. As they approached the dead whale in a dory, they discovered the waters were "swarming with sharks." A giant shark positioned himself between the dory and the whale. Captain Cramer opened fire with a 30-30 rifle, the muzzle of the rifle nearly touching the great white's head. After firing several rounds, the shark was stunned. The *Ollie S.* put the shark in tow and headed for Yaquina Bay. Eventually the shark came to and attempted to get loose. When the *Ollie S.* docked in Yaquina Bay, the great white was still alive. When the shark was hoisted out of the water it weighed in at about 5,000 pounds.

Captain Cramer told a local reporter that had he realized the shark was as big as it was, he never would have attempted its capture. Cramer planned to have the monster shark cured and mounted.[20]

END NOTES
1. Jack A. Bristol, "Oregon Soup Fin Shark Suddenly Found," *Oregonian*, 19 Jan. 1941.
2. Ibid.
3. "*Kingfisher* turns 50 on June 26," *News Guard*, 22 May 1991.
4. "Oregon Soup Fin Shark Suddenly Found."
5. Ibid.
6. "Local Boats Fishing Shark," *Newport Journal*, 20 Nov. 1940.
7. "Lions Fed Shark Meat at Abbey Banquet Wednesday," *Yaquina Bay News*, 28 Nov. 1940.
8. "Soup-Finners Need A Boat to Get Far," *Yaquina Bay News*, 20 Nov. 1941.
9. "The Leeward Side," *Yaquina Bay News*, 29 Nov. 1945.
10. "Fish Plants Making Improvements," *Newport Journal*, 12 March 1941.
11. "Fish Industry Employs 400," *Newport Journal*, 9 July 1941.
12. "*Kingfisher* turns 50."
13. "*Anna H* in Patrol Service," *Newport Journal*, 24 Sept. 1941.
14. "The Leeward Side," *Yaquina Bay News*, 31 Oct. 1946.
15. "Fish Plants Need Help," *Newport Journal*, 12 July 1944.
16. "Fish Canning Season Closes," *Newport Journal*, 19 Jan. 1944.
17. "Year Round Industry Steadily Gains in Newport Area," *Newport Beacon*, 2 Oct. 1941.
18. "128 Boats Fish for Tuna; One Trip Nets Men $1996 Check," *Yaquina Bay News*, 30 July 1942.
19. *Population Trends in Newport*, Bureau of Municipal Research and Service (University of Oregon, 1959).
20. "Big Man-Eating Shark Captured," *Yaquina Bay News*, 2 Oct. 1913.

This great white shark was captured by the Ollie S. off Yaquina Head in 1913. It weighed 5,000 pounds.

SOMETIMES A GREAT COMMOTION

When word got out that Paul Newman and his entourage had chosen Lincoln County as the setting for a seven-million-dollar motion picture called *Sometimes a Great Notion*, business as usual was put on hold.

Sometimes was the big-screen version of the novel written by Oregonian Ken Kesey. Paul Newman, Henry Fonda, Lee Remick, Michael Sarrazin, and Richard Jaeckel were cast as the central characters in the gripping story of the Stamper family: Oregon gypo loggers who battle a union and find themselves up against the entire town of Wakonda.[1]

Preliminary location work began in May 1970. The production crew members' first task was to build the Stamper home, which they hastily hammered together on the Siletz River at a cost of $150,000. It was but a shell with five or six coats of paint to make it look old. Set decorator William Kierman, who at the time had been nominated for six Academy Awards, filled the house with an eclectic mix of furnishings ranging from a seventeenth century monk's table to a chrome dinette set. Most of the furnishings were

Opposite: Filming Sometimes a Great Notion *on the Siletz River, where things turn ugly between a family of gypo loggers and a union.*

243

from Hollywood studios, but local antique shops such as Pandora's Box and Wilbur Prater's Museum rented out items for the filming. They received ten percent of the value of each article the first week and five percent each additional week. Old rolls of wallpaper found in the basement of Bateman's Furniture in Toledo were used to give an aged look to the hallway and bedrooms.[2] As the house neared completion, it was described as "a minor tourist attraction."

A more lucrative attraction appeared when it was announced as many as one hundred Lincoln County people would find work during the filming. Auditions com-

Set decorator and six-time Academy Award nominee William Kierman selected an eclectic mix of furnishings for the Stamper house, including some antiques rented locally.

244

menced a month later at Taft High School. A representative for Universal Studios was stationed at the Toledo branch of the unemployment office to interview loggers for bit parts in the film. Dean Fillmore, of Jepson Logging Company in Lincoln City, was hired as chief technical advisor and Paul Newman's stand-in for the dangerous scenes. Arrangements were made to shoot interior shots in the Newport Armory and many other locations throughout Lincoln County.

Soon celebrities began to take up temporary residence in Lincoln County. A front-page article in the *News-Times* reported the first sighting: Henry Fonda had been seen shopping in a Newport store.[3] Fonda, his wife, Shirlee,

The Stamper house was hastily constructed at a cost of $150,000. Designed merely as a Hollywood set, it had no foundation, plumbing, electricity, or functioning cupboards. These were added later by a succession of owners after the filming concluded.

and daughter Amy found lodging in a Salishan Spit home. Fonda, who knew nothing of logging, arrived two weeks before filming to familiarize himself with logging terms and equipment. He confided with a reporter that he worried about the sensitivities of a 200-year-old tree about to be felled.[4] In his spare time, Fonda also learned the finer points of agate hunting — so much so he purchased a rock tumbler to polish his beach findings.[5] Paul Newman, his wife, Joanne Woodward, their seven children, and their Irish wolf hound, Duffy, took refuge in a Salishan home.[6] Marlon Brando was sighted at Salishan when he paid a visit to Newman and actors Sam Gilman and Richard Jaeckel.[7]

Most of the locals were very familiar with the subject matter of the movie: logging. But the rigors of moviemaking probably took many by surprise. Coastal residents watched as truck after truck filled with sound and technical equipment wound its way up a hot, dusty logging road four miles east of Agate Beach for the filming of the logging scenes.[8] As quickly as they arrived, they packed up and moved on to the mud flats at South Beach to film the climactic scene in which Henry Fonda is injured by a log and Richard Jaeckel drowns. Filming was then shifted back to Agate Beach, then back yet again to South Beach to capture the tidal action when it was just right.[9] They discovered Yaquina Bay waters were too murky for filming, so prop men constructed a heated and filtered plywood tank for shooting the drowning scene. The logs in the tank were

bleached to maintain the clarity of the water. The log that Newman saws in an attempt to rescue Jaeckel was replicated using lightweight plywood.[10]

Tides and murky water were not the only environmental challenges the moviemakers faced. One scene requiring fog proved to be particularly costly. A studio representative was sent to Elk City to check on weather conditions. He phoned to report they were perfect. A 200-man crew quickly assembled and headed up the Yaquina River. By the time they arrived, the fog had burned off. A day and a half of filming was lost. They packed up again and headed for a logging set near Lincoln City.[11] One entire crew filmed scenes involving stars; yet another crew was used to

From left: Arthur Newman, Warren Merill, and Paul Newman discuss the filming of Sometimes a Great Notion *while on location at the Stamper house in summer 1970.*

Filming on Newport's Bayfront at the Bay Haven Inn Tavern, renamed "The Snag" for the movie. Mo Niemi, of Mo's Clam Chowder fame (at left), was an extra in the movie.

film "other scenes." Believe it or not, there was not enough rain or wind to suit their needs. A series of sprinklers (each with a separate control) was set up on top of the Stamper mansion on the Siletz. Pads to dampen the noise of the "rain" as it hit the roof were installed. A wind machine was also on standby.[12]

While the crews were on the move to locations all over the county, a two-bedroom suite at Newport's Dunes Motel, equipped with four telephones and a copy machine, remained the base of operations. The man in charge of logistics was Unit Manager Arthur Newman, Paul's brother. Arthur Newman and other behind-the-scenes personnel did their best to utilize as many local businesses as possible while filming. The entire wardrobe for the movie was purchased locally. One men's clothing store found itself depleted of stock when a studio representative walked in and purchased forty Pendleton shirts.[13]

While some merchants supplied the cast and crew with goods and services, others provided location. Several businesses on Newport's Bayfront and in Toledo were made part of Kesey's fictional town of Wakonda. Newport's Bay Haven Inn Tavern was transformed into the "The Snag" tavern. The modern tables at the Bay Haven were switched with rough wood ones so "it would look like a place where loggers would go."[14] One of the more well-known local extras used while filming in the Snag was Mo Niemi of Mo's Chowder House fame. Author Ken Kesey showed up unannounced during the filming at "The Snag" dressed in "a Mickey Mouse t-shirt and rumpled pants." Paul Newman invited the author to his dressing room for a chat. Kesey announced he would return and spent an entire day on the set. In Toledo, the Ross Theater (since torn down) and a union hall were utilized by the filming crew.[15]

Fourteen Hollywood stuntmen arrived at Fogarty State Park in July for filming a fight scene originally scheduled to be shot in "The Snag." (A climactic fight breaks out between the townspeople of Wakonda and the Stamper family.)[16] Despite the extra help, Paul Newman ended up with a broken ankle. The injury occurred when the starter on his motorcycle unexpectedly kicked back. Filming immediately ceased — Henry Fonda, Lee Remick, Michael

Sarrazin, and the filming crews and equipment left the area. It was estimated the broken ankle would drive production costs up about a half million dollars; luckily it was insured.[17]

Paul Newman's role in this motion picture was vital; not only did he star and co-produce the film, he was also its director. The movie's original director, Richard Colla, stepped down a week or two after principal photography began. Colla experienced a series of personality and/or creative differences with several cast members.[18] Newman, who had recently made his debut as a director in "Rachel, Rachel," which starred his wife, replaced Colla.[19]

Much to everyone's surprise, the cast and crew were back at work just a month after Newman's injury. When Newman paid a visit to his physician in Beverly Hills, it was discovered the star's fracture was not as serious as first thought.[20] Lee Remick had to return to Lincoln County almost as soon as she reached her London home.

Universal Studios publicist Harold Medelsohn announced to the local press that under Newman, the production was "extremely well-organized" and filming would probably end by the September 14, 1970, deadline.[21] The moviemaking commotion quickly died down as summer and filming drew to a close. The movie cast and crew soon became scarce. March of the following year marked a brief return of the film crew. The *News-Times* remarked, "Lincoln County took on the appearance of a Hollywood sound stage for a few days" while a production crew

(minus Fonda, Newman, Remick, and the other stars) filmed a few scenes needed for the opening title and credits. Much of this was done using a helicopter.[22]

All the moviemaking commotion produced two lasting treasures: a critically acclaimed movie that now makes for an enjoyable video rental; and the Stamper house. At the end of the filming, the house was slated for destruction.[23] A private party purchased the place even though it lacked plumbing, electricity, a foundation, and functioning cupboards. These were all added by a succession of owners. In the mid 1990s, the old Stamper house

Publicity print of Henry Fonda in his starring role. This print was signed by Paul Newman. (Universal Pictures)

was used as a fishing lodge.[24] Although once a movie set, this privately owned house remains a north Lincoln County landmark on Millport Slough. Fiction has become reality:

> *"... Rain drifts about the windows. Rain filters through a haze of yellow smoke issuing from the mossy-stoned chimney into slanting sky. The sky runs gray, the smoke wet-yellow. Behind the house, up in the shaggy hem of mountainside, these colors mix in windy distance, making the hillside itself run a muddy green . . ."* (from *Sometimes a Great Notion* by Ken Kesey).[25]

END NOTES
1. "Film Company Chooses County for Location," *News-Times*, 14 May 1970.
2. "Set Director Has Suggestions for Decorating Today's Homes," *News-Times*, 03 Sept. 1970.
3. "Film Company Starts Rehearsals at Taft High School," *News-Times*, 18 June 1970.
4. Connie Hoffman, "Henry Fonda Finds He's Really 'Cast' for "'Sometimes'," *News-Times*, 09 July 1970.
5. "Kesey Visits 'Snag' On Bayfront," *News-Times*, 23 July 1970.
6. "Film Company Chooses County."
7. Hoffman, "Tides, Rain Wait Not for Movie Makers," *News-Times*, 02 July 1970.
8. Hoffman, "Cameras Turn as Area Becomes Film Stage," *News-Times*, 25 June 1970.
9. "Tides, Rain Wait Not."
10. "Film Crew Moves, Shoots Scenes Along Siletz River," *News-Times*, 27 Aug. 1970.
11. "Henry Fonda Finds He's Really 'Cast.'"
12. "Logging Accidents

Filming of Sometimes a Great Notion *near Elk City, 1970.*

'Simple' Job For Movie Special Effects Crew," *News-Times*, 10 Sept. 1970.

13. "Film Producers Find County Folks Helpful," *News-Times*, 02 July 1970.

14. "Set Director Has Suggestions."

15. "Kesey Visits 'Snag'."

16. "Paul Newman Now Directing 'Sometimes'," *News-Times*, 30 July 1970.

17. "Filming May Resume Before End of Month," *News-Times*, 06 Aug. 1970.

18. Arthur S. Newman Jr., letter to author, 05 Sept. 1998.

19. "Paul Newman Now Directing."

20. Arthur S. Newman Jr.

21. "Movie Crews Return to County," *News-Times*, 13 Aug. 1970.

22. "Movie Crews Return For 'Credit' Shots For 'Great Notion'," *News-Times*, 25 March 1971.

23. "'Notion' Moves to Night Shooting; Film Nearing End," *News-Times*, 03 Sept. 1970.

24. "Former Movie Set to Become Fishing Lodge," *News-Times*, "Coast Tidings" section, Feb. 1994.

25. Ken Kesey, *Sometimes a Great Notion* (New York: Viking Press, 1964), 2.

Autographed publicity print of Paul Newman.
(Universal Pictures)

IMAGES

The following are the negative numbers for images that appear in this book. Some of the images have been digitally enhanced, but only to eliminate cosmetic defects caused by age or environment. Photographic prints may be obtained for a fee by contacting the Oregon Coast History Center at (541) 265-7509.

Page numbers appear on the left.

ROGER A. HART

CRUSTACEANS AND THE COLD WAR

THE FIGHTING, FISHING KINGFISHER

TO CATCH A SHARK

SOMETIMES A GREAT COMMOTION

IMAGES